KT-438-538

Coming to you
Live!

Behind-the-screen memories of forties and fifties Television

Collected and presented by
DENIS NORDEN
SYBIL HARPER
and NORMA GILBERT

Narrated by
DENIS NORDEN

METHUEN

791.45

45544

First published in Great Britain
by Methuen London Ltd
11 New Fetter Lane, London EC4P 4EE

Copyright © 1985 Denis Norden, Sybil Harper and Norma Gilbert
Composition words and music of 'Shell jingle' on page 186:
Copyright © 1959 Johnny Johnston

Filmset by Northumberland Press Ltd, Gateshead, Tyne and Wear
Made and printed in Great Britain
by Fletcher & Son Ltd, Norwich

British Library Cataloguing in Publication Data

Coming to you live! : behind-the-screen memories
    of forties and fifties television.
    1. Television broadcasting – Great Britain –
    History
    I. Norden, Denis   II. Harper, Sybil   III. Gilbert,
    Norma
    791.45′092′2   PN1992.3.G7

    ISBN 0-413-56020-1
    ISBN 0-413-56030-9 Pbk

STOCKTON-BILLINGHAM
LIBRARY
TECHNICAL COLLEGE

This book is available both
in hardback and paperback editions.
The paperback edition is sold subject to the condition
that it shall not, by way of trade or otherwise,
be lent, re-sold, hired out, or otherwise circulated
without the publisher's prior consent in any form
of binding or cover other than that in which
it is published and without a similar condition
including this condition being imposed
on the subsequent purchaser.

791.45
45544

Stockton & Billingham College

T018159

4 3 3 9 5 0 1 0 0 3 0 9 8 4 4 2 7 7 2 6 0 1 2

Coming to yc

ɔok is to be retur
ɔ last dat

Acknowledgments

Thanks are due to
Leonard Miall for
permission to use
material from
Radio 3 *In At The
Start* and to
TV Times for
permission to
reprint a section of
the Introduction.

Our special thanks
are due to Tony
Bridgewater, Cecil
Madden and
Geoffrey Strachan
for their encourage-
ment and advice.
     And, from one of
us, the customary
grateful nod to
Frank Muir.

Contents

List of Illustrations

The illustrations in this book have been collected and their subjects identified as a result of much patient and generous help from many individuals and organisations. Every effort has been made to describe the subjects and attribute picture sources correctly and trace copyright owners. Apologies are made for any errors and omissions.

Introduction

'Every night was a first night.'
DIANA PARRY *Production Assistant*

For most people the opposite of 'live' is 'dead'. For people concerned with the making of television programmes, the opposite is 'recorded'. Moreover, although the word 'live' has now more or less disappeared from television's vocabulary, during the period this book will be celebrating that was about the only way BBC and ITV programmes were transmitted: no re-takes, no out-takes, no second chances. If an actor in a television play made a mistake – if he fumbled his lines, or forgot them, or walked into the scenery, or lit his nose with a cigarette-lighter – the entire viewing audience were witnesses.

It was a period that began in 1936, when the BBC inaugurated the world's first regular high-definition television service. It lasted till the early sixties, when recording and editing techniques became effective enough to take over. By that time, television had covered the Coronation of King George VI in 1937; been shut down by the outbreak of war in 1939; re-opened in time for the 1946 Victory Parade; gained national acclaim in 1953 for its coverage of Queen Elizabeth's Coronation; and given birth to a commercial network in 1955. But even during ITV's first years, practically the only items which knew the security that comes from being recorded in advance were the commercials and newsreels.

Many viewers still cherish a favourite moment from the live television era. The one I remember with most affection occurred during an emotional drama, transmitted some time in the fifties, about a doctor in French colonial Africa who had recently left his wife in favour of somebody else's. However, while he was on his way up-river to a new life, an urgent message arrived from his former hospital. A virulent epidemic had just broken out locally – and guess who'd been

taken to the isolation ward as one of its first victims? Even if
you didn't manage to guess, the way they suddenly jumped
the doctor's face into close-up would have given you the tip-
off. His wife!

A pause for the commercial break – and doesn't that 'I
wonder where the yellow went' seem almost like a folk-song
at this remove? – then there we were in the isolation ward,
where the wife was lying on a narrow bed under one of those
ceiling-fans. (She wasn't Gwen Watford, but it would help
if you could mentally cast her in the part.) After the camera
had registered a few rather decorative plague-spots on her
cheeks, the door opened, and – this is the bit I've been leading
up to – in came the local priest.

He was played by a well-loved old character-actor whose
nimbus of fine white hair made him ideal for a far-flung
servant of the Church. Gazing down on her with concern, he
said, 'The sisters tell me you have lost the will to live.'

She shrugged. 'Nobody cares now whether I live or die.'

The priest shook his head in reproof. 'My child, there is
someone who always cares.'

'Who?' she said wearily.

And that's when it happened ... Over his face came the
familiar glazed look. As he stood there in his cassock and dog-
collar, clutching a battered prayer-book, you could actually
watch his mind chasing round in search of the elusive name.
Glazed turned into double-glazed, but – nothing. During that
ten seconds of complete silence, eternity took place.

Then, from somewhere off-screen, all of us at home heard
a hoarsely whispered monosyllable. The priest brightened.
'God,' he said, with so much relief in his voice that it went
up nearly an octave.

In television's early days, moments of that kind were so
frequently available that viewers came to regard them as one
of the medium's fringe benefits. More to the point, though,
their passing is still regretted even by programme-makers of
that period.

ALAN PROTHEROE *News Editor BBC Wales*
  So much of television now, it's cleaned up, it's adjusted,
  you don't see the gaffes. And that's actually taken a hell

of a lot out of TV. If somebody did something wrong then, they actually felt a sympathy for that human being. I think there was a much greater rapport between you and your audience in those days.

BIMBI HARRIS *Vision-mixer*
Of course, things always went wrong on live television.

MICHAEL BOND *Cameraman*
When I went in, it was still in the days of everything being tied up with string. I think all cameramen kept string in their pockets. It was still the three-camera set-up, and I can remember working on programmes where the cameras broke down one by one until you had none left and that was the end of television for the evening.

But it is not merely for its mishaps that the era of live television is still cherished by those who had a hand in putting programmes together. What has remained equally vivid in the memory is the excellence of some of those programmes; an excellence all the more satisfying because it was achieved with equipment, studio space and rehearsal time so woefully inadequate that, in those days, merely to get to the end of a programme felt like a victory against long odds.

And it was that aspect of live television which was remembered most fondly by those who faced our tape-recorders: the experience of working in an atmosphere of constant and cheerful improvisation, where every success was a triumph of resourcefulness over resources.

HAL BURTON *Drama Producer*
Nobody ever said to you, 'You can't possibly do that.' They said, 'Have a try and we'll see what we can do.'

RICHARD CAWSTON *Documentary Producer*
We were treading new ground all the time. Everything was new subject-matter, new styles.

RICHARD LEVIN *Designer*
> The great thing was that it was all so quick – if you had a disaster you had the opportunity next day to have three successes. Even if you had two disasters, it all just rolled along.

MICHAEL MILLS *Light Entertainment Producer*
> The thing people forget is the extraordinary smallness and tightness. Everybody in those days lived and worked within a few hundred feet of each other. It was the most extraordinarily tight little thing – tremendous camaraderie!

YVONNE LITTLEWOOD *Production Secretary*
> Everybody used to have a chance to do everything. There was no departmental thing.

CYRIL WILKINS *Cameraman*
> I always look back at those pioneering days as the best days of my life. It wasn't a job, it was a place to do work. A lot of us didn't take leave.

While that 'Bliss was it' glow probably warms the recollections of anyone who was in on the early days of a successful enterprise, the business of programme-making back in that live television era does seem to have been animated by something that no longer plays much of a part in the process. Whatever the something was – and guesses have ranged from 'a blend of audacity and dottiness' to 'a blind faith in the lash-up principle' – the speed at which the truth about it is now receding into the mists of television folklore prompted us to put together this collection of reminiscences.

They come from people with first-hand experience of those covered-waggon days: not only producers and directors from that time, but also cameramen, PAs, engineers, Floor Managers, scene-hands and dressers, as well as toilers concerned with such specialised matters as make-up, lighting, props, wardrobe, set-design and fire-prevention. (The description next to a contributor's name in the text denotes

his or her job at that particular time. Their subsequent television careers are outlined in the appendix on page 241.)

We are grateful to all of them for providing the material for
this book. We thank them for responding so readily, for
answering our solicitations so sympathetically and for per-
mitting us to submit their memories to such marathon jog-
ging. They have left us reasonably confident that while the
book may not represent an exact history of what happened in
that black-and-white era of television when practically every
programme was 'live', it is a fairly accurate record of what it
felt like. For that reason, all their contributions are apprecia-
ted, and most of their indiscretions have been respected.

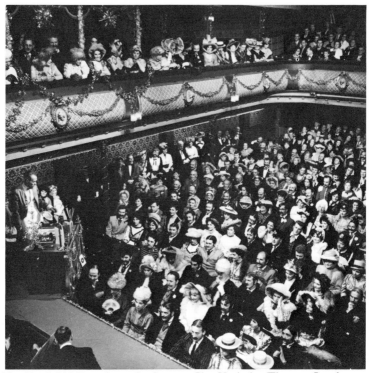

The Good Old Days from the famous City Varieties Theatre, Leeds

1 Light Entertainment

In those days they had a lot of variety shows –
old-fashioned variety, with the noise of the
band and all the excitement, jugglers,
magicians, the Television Toppers ... Sometimes
I think those things were better working on than
actually watching.
MICHAEL BOND *Cameraman*

My own parish during that springtime era of television was
the BBC's Light Entertainment Department. For much of
the time my boss was Eric Maschwitz, an enchanting man
who had written 'These Foolish Things' and 'A Nightingale
Sang in Berkeley Square' and was still convinced romance lay
in wait round the next corner. Tall, beaky and long-legged,
he loathed the term 'Light Entertainment' and would prowl
his office in shirt-sleeves and thin red braces enquiring,
'What is it meant to be the *opposite* of? Heavy Entertainment?
Or Dark Entertainment?'

The phrase also provided ammunition for visiting American colleagues, who enjoyed asking whether 'Light Entertainment' fell into the same insubstantial category as 'Light
Refreshments' or 'Light Housework'. It was not a question
that went down well on LE's factory-floor, which harboured
anxieties and ambitions every bit as desperate as those pre-
vailing in, say, the Drama Department. Moreover, some of
the programmes they generated would occasionally, if perhaps more rarely, turn out to be equally memorable.

GEORGE PETTICAN *Scene-hand*
I think one of the finest shows ever produced by the
BBC, bearing in mind everything in it was live, was a
series called *The Passing Shows*.

That series was produced by Michael Mills, known around
Lime Grove in my day as 'dark, satanic Mills', in tribute to
his Mephistophelian beard and deep-set eyes. Besides own-
ing a car that had the longest bonnet in the BBC car park, he
could also lay claim to being Light Entertainment's first
purpose-built producer.

Michael Mills: television's first LE producer

MICHAEL MILLS
Everybody else worked simply as 'producer, television', so you'd have a man like Michael Barry doing an Ibsen play one day and a variety show the next. Or Robert Barr would be writing a documentary while he was producing the Geraldo Concert Orchestra.

When I arrived on 4 January 1947, I was the first person to be appointed as 'producer, Light Entertainment' – something which, in the eyes of people who were already there and had been in the business far longer than me, immediately made me an expert. I hadn't been there more than three or four days when people like Michael Barry and George More O'Ferrall, who hated variety shows but kept getting given them, were coming into my office and saying, 'What shall I do with this show?'

To which I'd have to say, 'I'm sorry, but I really don't know. If it was being done in the theatre I'd put the items in this kind of running-order ... But other than that –'

'Oh, thank you, Michael, you've been a great help.' As I knew absolutely nothing about doing television, it was a case of the blind leading the short-sighted.

The Passing Shows was a series of five ninety-minute programmes Michael Mills devised in 1951 to reflect the history of popular entertainment from the turn of the century to its mid-point. Notably elaborate and fast-moving, it made use of as many as 105 sets per programme, which could be why some of the technicians he enlisted look back on the series with a respect that still contains traces of trepidation.

BEN PALMER *Engineer*
Those *Passing Shows* were really hectic. They had so many scene-changes that there was no room in the building for all the scenery to be stored at the same time. They would use a set, take it down, shift it outside, and start putting up another one while the action was taking place in some other set.

The wags had it that the scene-hands were sometimes taking down a set before it had actually been used in the transmission.

STEPHEN BUNDY *Designer*

Terrifying they were, those *Passing Shows*. The scene-boys had their shirts sticking to them.

FRANK HOLLAND *Assistant Property Master*

Those *Passing Shows* with Michael Mills – oh, we really worked hard on them. I'll give you some idea how hard: there were times when the props store at Lime Grove was actually filled from floor to ceiling with props for a *Passing Show*. Just one show ...

Of the five *Passing Shows* programmes, the one that seems to have etched itself most deeply in the collective folk-memory was a major study of the life and times of Marie Lloyd, with Pat Kirkwood playing the star part.

GEORGE PETTICAN *Scene-hand*

That Pat Kirkwood, she really was what I call a trouper; I only wish people could have seen how hard she worked in that *Passing Show*. She had so many changes of costume that there were three complete six-foot rails filled with clothes and we used bits of scenery to build a special quick-change dressing-room for her in Studio F, where they stored the sets. That poor girl, she was forever dashing in and out of there for costume changes, quite often stripping off on her way to do it, so that she was already half-naked by the time she got there. And when she had to dash back again for her next entrance, she'd still be putting on the new costume on her way to the set.

MICHAEL BOND *Cameraman*

I worked on that *Passing Show* about Marie Lloyd with Pat Kirkwood playing the part. At the end everybody on the set, including the scene-hands, applauded her.

Pat Kirkwood
as Marie Lloyd
in *Our Marie*,
1953

The performance caused such a stir that one of the big numbers from it was re-created in Coronation Year, when Bill Ward was given the task of putting on a special gala variety show in honour of the Queen's first visit to Lime Grove studios.

COLIN CLEWES *Cameraman*
I was on the camera while the Queen was sitting watching Pat Kirkwood sing 'My Old Man Said Follow The Van'. Pat moved a little bit to one side, so she could see the Queen better and the Queen would have a better view of her, but I automatically moved my camera, too – so as not to lose my best shot of her. She moved away again to get back into the Queen's eyeline, so again I moved my camera.

And that's how we went on right to the end of the song – her trying to place herself for the Queen, me determined to get the shot right. That was all I cared about, never mind the Queen.

That royal visit to Lime Grove included another event that set television tongues wagging. The Queen decided to use the occasion to bestow a knighthood on the then Director of Television, George Barnes.

CECIL MADDEN *Assistant Controller*

They chose my office to do it in. So all my montage photographs were taken off the walls and the place was converted into a sort of Palm Court. They also had a special dais built in the studio for the Queen to sit on when she went in there afterwards to watch the gala variety show. A lot of chairs were got out of the prop room and painted gold, which made them all look pseudo-period, pseudo-Louis, and also slightly red in colour.

Well, after Barnes had been given his knighthood, the entire party came into the studio and down they all sat on these special chairs – the Queen on the biggest one, Barnes on her left, and the Duke of Edinburgh on her right.

About halfway through the show – I think it was while Al Read was on – George Barnes's chair collapsed. Just collapsed. There was our newly knighted Director of Television suddenly sitting on the floor.

I was standing at the back and I saw the Queen clasp hold of her chair and look hard at both sides of it, as if to say, 'I could be on the floor next.' And she easily could have been. Those chairs were full of dry-rot, every one of them.

Although the content of some of those early LE programmes would be considered fairly naive nowadays, many of them went in for technical effects that were ambitious even by modern standards. Some of these become even more impressive when you bear in mind the limitations imposed by the camera-lenses to which they were confined. There was a period, for instance, when they could only achieve a close-up by pushing the camera forward to within inches of the subject.

VERA SETON-REID *Vision-mixer*

Eric Fawcett was producing a can-can routine with the Windmill girls and from the gallery he was telling a cameraman, 'In, in! Go in!'

We heard a little voice say, 'Mr Fawcett, if you have that camera track in any more, I'll have you up for rape.'

The Windmill Girls, at Alexandra Palace, 1946

Eric Fawcett, one of LE's most reliable producers, had been Jack Buchanan's understudy before the War and in moments of private elation would still execute a creditable soft-shoe.

But the lack of a zoom was not the only problem that bedevilled cameras in those days. Cameramen had to accommodate themselves to heavy cables that constantly needed to be kicked out of their path and a view-finder which showed them the picture upside-down and the wrong way round.

COLIN CLEWES *Cameraman*

When the picture in your camera view-finder used to be upside-down and left-to-right reversed, once you'd got your head stuck in there it was strange how soon you got used to it. Everything reversed itself in your mind and you would quite automatically pan in the reverse direction. In fact, one of the worst moments I ever had was with a parrot. I had a big close-up of it and for some reason I can't remember now I took my head out of the camera for a moment. When I looked back into the view-finder I got quite a shock, because the parrot looked right-way up. What had happened, of course, was that it had swung round and was now hanging upside-down.

CYRIL WILKINS *Cameraman*

Just before Christmas I was on a circus programme in Studio B with Koringa, who finished her act by climbing a ladder made out of swords and, to cap it all, she had this blooming ten-foot python. They put the python in a clothes-basket in the corner of the studio but due to the heat and the lighting it got rather frisky and got out. I was told afterwards that the circus people saw this thing but knowing it was harmless they didn't take any notice of it.

Well, we didn't know it was harmless and I can remember taking a shot of Koringa walking up this ladder made of swords, then looking down and there was this blooming great snake. It went under my dolly and across the floor to where one of the boom operators was. And he, thinking it was a camera cable – which they used to kick out of the way in those days – he gave this snake a kick. And when he saw what he'd kicked, he dropped his earphones and ran. At which, everybody scattered.

Koringa with one of her crocodiles

There were also shades of white which those cameras were unable to cope with, while certain lighting conditions would induce a phenomenon known as 'peeling'.

DON GALE *Cameraman*

In Studio H at Lime Grove, there was an EMI camera which was known as the CPS, and the peculiarity of that one was that if you got a sudden bright light in it, the picture used to explode, or 'peel', as we called it. We had an artist on once with a monkey, a chimpanzee it was, and for transmission this chimpanzee came on wearing a jacket with all sequins over it that sparkled. We coped with it till the very, very last moment of the act, when the monkey took a sort of bow. A bit of light off the sequins went into the camera lens and, poof, it 'went'. After the programme, the BBC was swamped with calls from mothers saying their children had gone into hysterics – how dare we blow up the chimp?

MICHAEL BOND *Cameraman*

Being a cameraman was a unique job because of the way it made you use all your senses. You had someone saying something in one ear of your headphones, someone else saying something in the other; your right hand was focusing, your left hand on the panning handle, and at the same time your feet were being used for signalling. It made demands on all your faculties.

BEN PALMER *Engineer*

There was a show called *Dreamer's Highway*, with Johnny Brandon, where the cameras needed so much light on the set that the heat from the lamps blew the sprinkler system. Watching the rehearsal up in the gallery, during the afternoon, I said, 'That's funny. It looks like it's raining.' Before they could get the water turned off, the whole studio was flooded.

VIC GARDINER *Cameraman*

In the heyday of the big band shows, Bill Ward was known as the fastest-cutting director in the business. He produced one series of programmes called *Band Parade*, Cyril Stapleton I think it was, and we cameramen used to dread it, because he would cut on almost every bar of music. That meant the four cameras would be nothing but whirling lenses, because we didn't have zooms in those days, we just had to keep swinging our lenses round on their turret-mountings.

We spent the whole show praying we wouldn't get caught between one lens and another.... A great challenge.

BOB SERVICE *Cameraman*

I was a very new cameraman and it was my first time working on a dolly – meaning there was a man behind the camera pushing me around and I had to make signals to him when I wanted to track closer into the set or be pulled out from it.

My first shot was of a singer dressed up as a miner, complete with helmet and Davy Lamp, and the plan was that as he got towards the end of his song, I would gradually track out to get a long shot of him. That may sound simple, but as I say it was my first attempt and it entailed 'pulling focus' – in other words, compensating for the fact that as I moved, the distance between the singer and my camera-lens would gradually be increasing.

I made the signal to my tracker to start pulling me out – in those days, it was a raised forefinger pointing backwards – and prepared to alter focus as I saw the singer getting further away. But nothing happened. I thought the tracker hadn't seen my signal, so I did the pointing backwards forefinger again. Still nothing. I risked taking a look away from the view-finder for a second, and discovered we were actually moving. So why wasn't the shot of the singer changing?

Well, by that time, we'd got to the end of the song, so I took my head out of the view-finder – and there was the miner still exactly the same distance from me. He'd thought my signal had been to beckon him towards me, so as fast as we'd been moving backwards he'd been walking forward.

It undermined my confidence about coping with a tracking camera no end.

DEREK BURRELL-DAVIS *Producer*

I did what was, at that time, the longest tracking shot ever – down a line of violinists while they were playing some light classical piece. But the point is, we only actually had four violinists there, because that's all I could afford.

The shot was achieved by making a diagonal line across the studio and starting them all up in one corner. I began on violinist Number One, then I went to Number Two and, as I moved to Number Three violinist, Number One came round to be Number Five, then Two became Six, and so on. And they kept doing this until we arrived at the wall on the other side of the studio. All done live, remember.

STEPHEN BUNDY *Designer*

There was a period when one camera could be pointing straight at another without your being able to see it on screen because it would be so out-of-focus. I remember a funny old thing we did with Henry Caldwell called *Café Continental*, where there was a circular audience with the acts going on in the middle. But because of the camera's limited depth of field all you could ever see of them behind the acts was just a sort of blur.

Studio A at Alexandra Palace set-up for *Café Continental*

Then they moved the show into Studio G at Lime Grove where the cameras were different and I got a panic telephone call from Ronnie Waldman, then head

Café Continental: Hélène Cordet with compère Père Auguste showered
with champagne at the end of the show

of Light Entertainment. 'I say, you must do something.
We're seeing all those *faces*! Put a gauze in front of them
or something.' He thought that was really terrible,
couldn't stand it.

Café Continental seems to be one of those variety programmes
which have unaccountably lodged themselves in viewers'
memories while similar, and possibly worthier, shows have
disappeared without trace. One reason may have been its
regular opening and closing sequences which were of a dottiness that certainly approaches the unforgettable.

JOHN SUMMERS *Cameraman*
> At the start of each programme, the camera would be
> looking out from inside the window of a hansom-cab
> that was just drawing up outside the café. A flunkey
> would come forward, open the cab door, bow to the lens
> – 'Good evening, sir, good evening, madame' – then the
> camera would take us inside the café where old Père
> Auguste, with his little white beard, would be standing
> to bid you welcome. It was the most incredibly compli-
> cated series of shots for a live show. . . . And we never
> once got it right.
>
> At the end of the programme, the whole series of shots
> would be done in reverse. The camera would slowly pull
> back from the café door, the flunkey would salute the
> lens – 'Goodnight, sir, goodnight madame' – he'd open
> the hansom-cab door, the camera would pull back inside
> it, then a female hand wearing a long white glove would
> come forward and pull down the cab window-blind
> which bore the caption 'The End'. That's the shot that
> always gave me hysterics, because who did they choose
> to do that gloved hand? Believe it or not, it was always
> some beefy scene-hand.

Most people we questioned about what it was like to work
behind a camera in those days brought up the name of one
cameraman who now seems to have acquired an almost
legendary status. Known first for his habit of always covering
his camera with a black cloth, his most notable achievement
was with a drama producer named Fred O'Donovan, whose
strongly held view that there was no real necessity for what
he called 'continually cutting about from camera to camera'

Jasmine Bligh (*right*) Ted Langley with pre- and post-war cameras

was given dramatic emphasis in the early fifties when he produced a ninety-minute live play that was shot on one camera only.

Its cameraman, for whom the skills and concentration required must have been fearsome, was Ted Langley.

MICHAEL MILLS *Producer*

Ted was unbelievable. He really did know all there was to know and no one could argue with him. I had had one or two brushes with him where he'd had the best of me. Then one day I described to him a shot I wanted and Ted said, 'It can't be done.' He wouldn't be budged. 'No, no, sorry. It can't be done.'

I thought it could, so I said, 'Ted, if you can't do it, I can.'

He said, 'Right. You come down here then, Michael. Let's see you do it.'

I said, 'I'm on my way.' And as I went down that ladder to the studio floor I was sort of praying to myself, 'Oh, Christ, I hope I can do this. I hope I can get it right.

Because if I do, I'll have the measure of Ted Langley.'

Anyway, I got on to the camera and I did it. I was able to step off and say, 'There you are, Ted.' I might mention, between you and me, it was entirely good luck that I managed it, because I really had no camera technique. I just knew what I wanted.

The studio didn't exactly break into applause, but I could feel a sort of movement in my favour.

CYRIL WILKINS *Cameraman*

Ted Langley and I were rivals at one time. There often used to be a pianist doing a late-night programme and it became a game between us to see which one could get shots the other hadn't thought of. You'd start over his left-hand shoulder, go over to the right, along the keyboard, round into the crook of the piano, anything.

I had a very good man pushing my dolly at that time, so one Sunday we did every possible angle. We went right round the piano, even shooting back towards the control gallery, which was in the darkness so you couldn't see it. I said, 'I bet Ted won't beat that.'

Next Sunday I was watching because Ted was on the show and I saw him get a shot of the piano pedals. I sent him a little note, 'You win.' I never thought of the feet.

During the early years of both BBC and ITV, the Light Entertainment departments served as a kind of combined training-ground and firing-range. On both channels, the sheer volume of LE's output of live programmes placed responsibilities on its employees that tended either to make or break.

SHEELAGH REES *Production Secretary*

At the beginning a lot of small programmes had to be made, ten-minute ones, and nobody wanted to be doing those programmes forever, so each producer – we didn't have directors then – would do them in turn for two weeks. They were what we called our austerity fortnights.

There was very little advance planning; we'd have

The rivals: (*above*) cameraman Ted Langley; (*below*) cameraman Cyril Wilkins

somebody with a puppet one day, next day someone playing the piano, or someone singing. The producer I was working with said he had to look in the newspaper every morning to see what he was doing that night.

JOAN KEMP-WELCH *Producer, Associated-Rediffusion*
My PA and I used to do a programme in the morning, rehearse one in the afternoon for the next day, do all the paperwork in the evening, and back the next morning. Goodness, we worked.

DEREK BURRELL-DAVIS *Producer*
With Ronnie Taylor, who was a famous radio producer and writer in the north, we did a programme from Manchester called *Music Box* where we didn't have a set designer and we hadn't got any sets. All we had were bits and pieces that were still lying around from the days when the place had been a film studio. There was one archway-piece I found that I kept painting and re-painting, using it in every possible position – sideways, upside-down, any old way.

I can remember doing the song 'Stage Coach' using just a singer and a pile of old prop baskets. The singer simply sat on top of the baskets, holding a pair of reins which went down out of shot to a property man below who kept gently pulling on them. At the same time, other prop men pushed against the baskets, making them sway and creak just like a carriage going along. Done against black drapes, the effect was stunning.

SHEELAGH REES *Production Assistant*
We PAs used to choose the scenery for those bits-and-pieces programmes, because there were no designers or production managers.

If you were in doubt you'd go to the man in charge of scenery stock and say, 'We've got this pianist coming, what set do you think we should have?'

And he'd say, 'Well, I think I'd have the ivory drawing-room if I were you', and we'd say thankfully, 'Yes, the ivory drawing-room, of course.'

There would be a studio-plan of the scenery and we'd

have to make six copies of it, because there were no photocopiers in those days. One poor girl put one of her carbons in the wrong way round and the set was put up back-to-front and at the wrong end of the studio. The lighting man couldn't light it and it all had to be taken down and re-done very quickly just before transmission. I saw this poor girl in the canteen and she was in tears.

I think we had too much responsibility in those days. I think I had more responsibility than I have ever had since.

BILL WARD *Producer*

That first ITV weekend I produced a programme on the Friday night, I did a *Saturday Spectacular* the following night, went straight from that to the Embassy Club to act as an additional Floor Manager for Henry Caldwell who was producing a late-night programme there with Ron Randell, and the next day I went into the Palladium for the first *Sunday Night at the London Palladium*.

DENIS FORMAN *Producer*

I was the producer of *Chelsea at Nine*. That was a large-scale international variety show that went out live on Mondays at nine o'clock from the Chelsea Palace.

The working week was fairly incredible. We used to finish the show at ten o'clock and it took about an hour and a half to wrap everything up. We'd have a drink and finish about one in the morning, then I'd drive home and get to bed about two or three.

Tuesday morning we'd have a post-production meeting at 11 a.m., get out a running-order for the next Monday, then start phoning all round the world to check up on our artistes, most of whom would be flown in from Europe or even the USA. By Wednesday you hoped you knew what you had in the next show, although by the Saturday you were often still short of an act.

The first rehearsal would take place on Saturday morning with the people who'd arrived in the country and Sunday morning there'd be a band-call. Another rehearsal was held on Sunday afternoon with whatever costumes and scenery you'd been able to assemble.

Sunday nights you'd find yourself in hotel rooms all over London, listening to your visiting artistes run through their repertoire, usually with piano accompaniment, and there'd be difficult evenings when important people, like Callas, would not agree to cut out anything and would only agree to come on the show if they could sing for fifteen minutes; which was longer than the public wanted to hear even Callas in that type of variety show.

So Sunday was generally a late night and Monday morning you started on a stagger-through rehearsal, with a proper dress-rehearsal in the afternoon which you got through by six or seven o'clock, if you were lucky. Then everybody was called for eight-thirty and we went on air at nine.

Of course, once videotape and recording came in, you could shoot the acts one at a time if you wanted to; you didn't have that difficult business of getting everybody in the same place at the same time and doing their thing right first time.

Joan Kemp-Welch in the control gallery with vision-mixer (*left*) and her PA (*right*)

JOAN KEMP-WELCH *Producer*

When I started in Associated-Rediffusion the studio we used was so small and had such a low ceiling it wasn't even considered large enough to take *still* photographs in. But, believe it or not, we did morning programmes every day out of that studio. All sorts of programmes. We did personality programmes, we did twenty-minute revues, we did cooking, shopping, medical programmes – I even had Ram Gopal and his ballet in there.

It was from those programmes I learnt how to make sets look enormous when they really consisted of nothing, using tricks like painting the floor. I also learnt how attractive fruit and vegetables could look on television if you shot them in big close up.

Later, when I did a programme which became very famous, *Cool for Cats*, in which I illustrated records with dancers and visuals, I often used to do it by cutting

Cool for Cats dancers

to big close-ups of fruit and so on, which was a direct crib from those cooking programmes.

Joan Kemp-Welch's *Cool for Cats* was a landmark series in live LE, introducing notions in design and camerawork that made use of perspective, mirrors, painted floors, and multiple-picture effects. It was probably the most notable example of the way imaginative improvisation could overcome deficiencies in budget and back-up facilities. But not always.

RICHARD LEVIN *Designer*

I was the designer on one of Bill Cotton's early productions. It was called *The Show Band Show*, and I had this notion of introducing its title by having the band sit on three tiers, which would have the words:

SHOW

BAND

SHOW

picked out in lights. It was a great idea, but on rehearsal the cameraman taking the shot couldn't pull back far enough for some reason. So all Bill could see of the show's title was:

HOW

AND

HOW

BILL COTTON *Producer*

There was one show, whose producer I suppose had better remain anonymous, where they had a stream with real water that had a little bridge over it on which a girl was to sing some kind of sentimental number. Well, on the last rehearsal, the producer decided that what would really complete the picture was a swan floating by as the girl sang. So they got hold of a very life-like rubber swan and a scene-hand was detailed to push it off into the stream at a given cue.

But, of course, it being a live show, he got a bit too enthusiastic and instead of gently pushing it, he gave the thing such a shove that it turned over and went head downwards. So that was the romantic picture the viewers received: a girl singing a sentimental song on a rustic bridge, while below her a swan slowly floated by upside-down ...

Something else the trail-blazers of both ITV and BBC can claim to have shared was a certain inadequacy in the accommodation they were expected to inhabit. In terms of discomfort, there seems to have been little to choose between Alexandra Palace and Associated-Rediffusion's headquarters at Kingsway.

MICHAEL MILLS *Producer*

Outside the window of my office at Alexandra Palace was a sort of glass roof and what I can only describe as a pile of rubbish. About every six months a man in a brown coat would arrive with a notebook and say, 'Any rats or mice?' We'd say, 'Yes, there are', and he'd make a note in his book and go away.

I never discovered whether he was there to make a census, exterminate them or even breed them.

BIMBI HARRIS *Vision-mixer*

There were no loos initially at Kingsway, so we had to go to Holborn underground station and they paid us a loo allocation for our pennies in the slot. We were also allowed a hairdressing allocation, because of the filth from the builders being there, and the men were given a cleaning allowance for their suits.

JIM POPLE *Film Editor*

When they built the Preview Theatre at Kingsway, the eight holes in the wall for the projectors were three feet from the ground. The builders had the plan upside-down – they should, of course, have been three feet from the ceiling.

VICKI MILLER *Production Assistant*

There was a man in an office along the corridor and we always used to say 'Good morning' to him, but none of us knew who he was or what he did. He was there for about six months, then he suddenly disappeared.

We subsequently discovered he'd just walked in the building, found an office with a telephone and taken it over. He was nothing to do with Rediffusion at all.

BILL WARD *Producer*

The start of ITV was very much like BBC, very much back to pioneering.

Before leaving the BBC for ITV, the protean Bill Ward had been producing Vic Oliver's *This Is Show Business*, plus a fortnightly alternation of Arthur Askey's *Before Your Very Eyes* and Terry-Thomas's *How Do You View?*, as well as a once-a-month presentation of *The Hit Parade*, a forerunner of *Top of the Pops*. All of them broke new ground in Light Entertainment and now he was about to set another precedent with *Sunday Night at the London Palladium*.

BILL WARD

On the first Sunday we did the Palladium show, we finished the last dress-rehearsal before we went on air, and Lew Grade got very worried about a problem we ran into getting the set for *Beat the Clock* up in time. We had two and a half minutes to do it in, and the first time the stage-staff tried it they took fifteen minutes. The second try we got it down to ten, and they gradually reduced it, but the best we had it down to on that final rehearsal was about five minutes. Lew called me in from the control van in a great panic and said, 'You just won't be able to make it.'

Sunday Night at the London Palladium: Bill Ward with Tommy Trinder and Marie Wint

I said, 'We'll do it,' but he said, 'No, no, some big changes have got to be made.'

I said, 'Don't worry. It'll be all right. It's a toughie, but the boys will work on it.'

The thing was, we were using the Palladium stage-staff and I knew they were the best there were. They'd been there for years, and the way they handled their job, the way they handled the influx of TV crews – I knew I was working with the cream of the theatre. So I said to Lew, 'We'll manage it.'

But Lew was in a real flap about it. He said, 'No, you won't.'

I said, 'Look, Lew, let's have a bet on it. If we make the set-change satisfactorily and on time, will you pay for a marvellous weekend in Paris?'

He said, 'Yes.'

I said, 'Does that include Frank Beale?' He was the Floor Manager, attached to the Palladium's own stage manager, Jack Matthews. 'A marvellous weekend in Paris for both of us?'

He said, 'Yes, yes.'

So I went down to Frank and I said, 'You're in on this,' and told him about the bet. Then I said, 'What's going wrong?'

He said, 'Just that the boys aren't used to it yet. It'll be all right, though. It'll take us all of the two and a half minutes but we'll make it.'

And sure enough, on the night, he came through. Everything was done in time. And Lew was also as good as his word. He booked us into the George V, in the penthouse suite. Frank and I went across there and had a marvellous weekend.

Unfortunately, not all remembered 'firsts' ended so auspiciously, nor was self-confidence always so satisfyingly justified.

BILL COTTON

The first big show I produced was with Frank Chacksfield and what seemed to me then an enormous orchestra. I'd never done that kind of forty-five-minute live programme before, so I asked Yvonne Littlewood, who was Francis Essex's PA at the time, to sit in the gallery and just sort of keep an eye on me.

On rehearsal, it was all going along fine till we came to a number called 'The Wedding of the Painted Doll', when somehow I began getting my shots all out of sequence. The only pictures we were taking were of the musicians, but it was quite a complicated arrangement and I'd find myself on a violinist when the flautist was playing, and I'd get to the flautist when a drummer was hitting.

Well, because I was very new and not terribly experienced, I just found everything inside me going blank. I thought, 'God, this is terrible.' It felt like the world had come to an end.

Then I heard this angelic voice in my ear. I say angelic, because it really was like receiving help from above. It said, 'Get them to play it once again and record it on tape. Then send them all to tea and listen to it with your camera-script in front of you. You may find you can simplify things a bit.'

With enormous aplomb I got straight through to the studio. 'Tell you what,' I said. 'What we'll do is play it once more and we'll record the music. Then we'll all go to tea.'

It was Yvonne, of course, and during tea the two of us sat together with my camera-script and cut it so that it worked. She's great, Yvonne. Takes enormous pains, very, very good with pictures, and she's not only one of the genuine pioneers of television, she's maintained the standard all through and is still ahead of most people.

MICHAEL MILLS *Producer*

The first weekly half-hour situation-comedy was called *Family Affairs*, all about a middle-class family, the Conovers, living in Northwood. Eric Maschwitz wrote it, it was all done in one set at the back end of Studio B at Alexandra Palace and it went out live on Saturday nights. I did thirteen weeks of it and it nearly killed me. It nearly did for Eric, too. You'll understand why when I tell you the way we used to have to do it.

After five days of outside rehearsal we'd go into the studio on the Saturday morning and rehearse it from 10.30 a.m. till 1.30 in the afternoon. Then we'd have to knock off and go home because, owing to other programming commitments, there'd be a gardening programme or something going on up the other end of the studio. Then at eight o'clock that night we'd come back and transmit it.

I remember that so well. The first-ever sit-com, and every Saturday we'd get three hours to rehearse it. A half-hour show going out that evening!

JOAN KEMP-WELCH *Producer*

I did the first programme after the Guildhall ceremony that officially opened Independent Television. It was the following morning, and the programme was called *How to Make a Frame of Flowers*. We did it from the Viking Studio and David Boisseau, the ex-BBC director who'd trained me, stood behind me in the gallery. I was so nervous that when we came to the very end of it and I had to say, 'Fade Camera One', I couldn't think of the words. I can remember David leaning forward and saying, 'Fade Camera One.'

MAGGIE SAUNDERS *Assistant Floor Manager*

Walton Anderson was the producer on one of the very first post-War variety shows and he'd booked a balalaika player he'd seen playing in a London club. Unfortunately, this guy couldn't speak any English so when Leslie Jackson, the Floor Manager, gave him the cue to play, he just looked at Leslie and smiled benignly.

Well, that got Leslie a bit worked up because it was all going out live and he had Walton shouting in his earphones, 'Cue him, cue him!' So Leslie started to mime playing the balalaika ... At which this chap laughed himself sick and leaned back in his chair applauding. And he carried on applauding for about ten seconds, during which we were all having mini heart-attacks in the gallery.

Well, of course, he finally caught on to what they wanted him to do. But till he did, the camera had nothing to do except stay on a chap who was sitting there mysteriously applauding something viewers were unable to see.

JOAN MARSDEN *Floor Manager*

The very first show I did was *International Music Hall*. They sent me in a chauffeur-driven car to London airport to meet what was called a 'speciality' act, a troupe of ten tumblers. And when we got to the theatre, I'd lost one of them; I only had nine. And, of course, he *would* be the one who held the whole lot up ...! We searched all over but there was no trace of him. Then, thank goodness, just in time for the live show, we got word he'd turned up in some funny embassy somewhere.

BRIAN TESLER *Producer*
For my first year and a bit in Light Entertainment I did nothing but panel-games – 'quiz-games' as they were then called – starting with a disastrous one called *Why?* It was based on a not very good idea involving adult panellists pretending to be children and parents. The one being the child had to ask *Why?* to every statement the parent made, the idea being to try and flummox one or the other. It was put on at peak-time, and as it was the first show to take over the spot that had been occupied by the phenomenally successful *What's My Line?*, it was probably doomed from the start. After the first programme, the switchboard was *inundated* with calls to take it off.

That was the mid-fifties period when the creative resources of the entire nation seemed to be directed towards finding a successor to *What's My Line?* Among the variations tried and found wanting were such radical alternatives as *Guess My Story, Guess My Secret, Find The Link, Know Your Partner, The Name's the Same, Ask Your Dad, One of the Family, Music, Music, Music, What Do You Know?* and *Where on Earth?* Many of them subsequently re-emerged over the years while some, their titles suitably updated, are still in service today.

It was during those years that Frank Muir and I, in our capacity as LE consultants, were entrusted with producing the 'pilot' for a new panel-game idea with the promising title of *Who's Whose?* It was based on the fact that most people who find themselves in the presence of a room full of strange couples will indulge in the mental game of pairing them up. Which of the women is that man's wife? Which man belongs to the lady over there?

The format had a man ('Mr X') seated in front of three women, referred to as Mrs A, Mrs B and Mrs C. A panel, made up of a psychiatrist, a clergyman, an agony aunt and the mandatory showbiz celebrity, had to try to work out which of the women was actually Mrs X. To do this they were first allowed an 'instinctive' guess, based solely on their first look at the quartet, then they were permitted to ask each of the four a limited number of non-specific questions, after which they made a reasoned guess.

The Name's the Same: (left to right) Brenda Bruce, Frank Muir, Catherine Boyle, Denis Norden; 1959

There were two interesting results. The first was that the panel were much more frequently correct in their instinctive reaction than they were in the answers they worked out as a result of shrewd questioning.

The second was that after playing a series of games, some with the genders reversed – i.e. three men and one women – there was only one instance in which both the instinctive and the reasoned answers of the entire panel came to the same unanimous conclusion: namely, that Mr X was married to Mrs C.

In the event, he turned out to be married to Mrs A. But that wasn't what put paid to the programme. What killed it was that while we were all having drinks in the hospitality room afterwards, Mr X and Mrs C were observed not merely moving blindly towards each other but subsequently cosying up in no uncertain manner.

Tom Sloan, head of Light Entertainment at the time, made it known there and then that the BBC dare not have anything to do with the game. Nor would he budge from that position when Frank and I suggested changing the title to *Who* Was *Whose?*

Finally, in 1955, the LE Department sent out an SOS to viewers, asking them to make their own suggestions for a suitable panel-game to replace *What's My Line?* Eighty-six people proposed a show entitled *What's My Sideline?*

CYRIL WILKINS *Cameraman*
>We used to do *What's My Line* in the old TV Theatre before it was refurbished properly and it used to get very hot in there. I was the show's technical manager on an occasion when Gilbert Harding, who suffered terribly from the heat, asked if we could turn the lights down a bit. I told the lighting chap to turn the key-light down during rehearsal, but when it came to transmission he put the thing up full again. You could see Gilbert sweating, and next thing we knew, he took his jacket off. And there he was in his white shirt, whose effect on the camera was to make his face turn completely black.

BOB SERVICE *Cameraman*
>Rediffusion's game shows, like *Double Your Money* and *Take Your Pick* were a novelty at that time because they gave away expensive prizes, which the BBC didn't stoop to. We had cases like the dustman who won a complete set of the *Encyclopaedia Brittanica*. I've kicked myself ever since that I didn't offer him £10 for it.
>
>Another famous one was the little old lady who won a Lotus sports car in kit form. It came in a box.

BRIAN TESLER *Producer*
>There was an early-fifties panel-game called *Guess My Story* where the regular panellists were Pat Kirkwood, Helen Cherry and Michael Pertwee, and in the fourth seat we'd always have a guest-panellist.

One memorable Thursday the guest was Gerald Kersh, the novelist. He was fine at the rehearsal, but during the break before the actual show I was eating in the canteen and the Make-up lady came in and said she'd just been in to make Gerald Kersh up and he was absolutely pie-eyed. This was an hour before we were due to go on the air live.

I got hold of Larry and Pauline Forrester, our researchers – he's now a screen-writer in Los Angeles – and sent them over to sober him up. They poured black coffee down him, walked him up and down, just like in the movies, and took him out for some fresh air, but it didn't help. I had him sitting between Helen Cherry and Pat Kirkwood and though they tried as hard as they could to find the answers in the thirty seconds of questioning each panellist was allowed – so that I could skip putting the camera on Kersh – it didn't always work. When the bell went and I had to go to him, he'd say something like, 'Whosh shosh a person was it?' All I could do was move straight to the next panellist. In his fuddled way, he was obviously aware that all he was getting was about three seconds each time, but luckily he couldn't quite make out what was happening and we managed to get through to the end of the show.

That was where each panellist said a good-night to the audience, but as we cut to Gerald Kersh for his the sound went absolutely dead. I yelled, 'We've lost sound – what's happened?' But by then we were off the air and the sound supervisor came in and said, 'I'm awfully sorry, there wasn't time to check with you, but when the camera got to Gerald Kersh the way he leaned forward into his microphone I thought he was going to say something bad, so I switched his mike off.'

I thanked him, went down to the studio floor, and when I got down there everyone was aghast, because they thought what Kersh had said had gone out. He'd leaned forward and said, 'I just want to say I would have been much better in this programme if it hadn't been for my attack of worms.'

That kind of dicing with disaster characterised many of our contributors' recollections of live LE. But although it may have been a department whose successes seemed to depend on makeshift and miracles, it did bring its members into a favoured relationship with many of the more glittering entertainers of the period.

VIC GARDINER *Cameraman*

The Arthur Askey show was the one where you always found an unusual number of scene-hands up in the lighting gantry above the studio. We couldn't understand their sudden interest in lighting till we realised you could look down from there straight into the quick-change room used by that remarkable lady, Sabrina.

Arthur Askey
with Sabrina

CHARLES BEARD *Fireman*

Controlling crowds at the Wood Green Empire was part of my job. When we had Johnny Ray, who was a number one American heart-throb at the time, all the teenagers used to flock round in hundreds and plead with me just to let them have a look at his dressing-room. With Cliff Richard, they offered me money one time just to let them kiss the phone that he used.

BARNEY COLEHAN *Producer*

The theatre we used for *The Good Old Days*, the City Varieties, Leeds, was very small and though that was part of the beauty of it the dressing-rooms were like little shoe-boxes. When Eartha Kitt came along to do her first programme there, everybody was rather in awe of this strange lady in dark glasses and leopard-skin coat, so I took her into this tiny dressing-room where there was hardly room for one person to turn round, and I apologised for it.

I said, 'I'm sorry it's not like the dressing-rooms you must be used to in Hollywood, but it's the best we have. The only thing I can say in its favour is that it may be small, but it was once used by Charlie Chaplin.'

Then I went down to carry on with the rehearsal and Eartha's daughter, a little girl about twelve then, came and sat in the stalls. I went over to her and said, 'How's your mother?'

She said, 'Oh, she's in floods of tears.'

I said, 'Well, I'm terribly sorry but there's nothing we can do, that's the best dressing-room we've got.'

'Oh, it's not a question of that,' she said. 'Charlie Chaplin is her idol and the fact that she's in the same dressing-room he used to have, you'll never get her out.'

MAGGIE SAUNDERS *Assistant Floor Manager*

There was a very early *Black and White Minstrel Show* from the TV Theatre whose opening shot had Leslie Crowther, dressed up as a baby, hanging high above the stage by a wire. It was in the days before programmes ran strictly to time and on this occasion the preceding programme overran. So we had the poor lad dangling up there for quite a while.

First of all he was laughing and gagging about it with the audience but after about five minutes he got quieter, because the wire was going back and forwards and he was beginning to feel a bit queasy. After about ten minutes he began to look really white, but we daren't let him down in case the previous programme came to an end suddenly and we didn't have time to re-hook him and haul him up there again.

It was fifteen minutes altogether before we got on the air and by that time we really thought he was going to pass out. The theatre audience, who couldn't see his discomfort, thought it was all great fun.

STEWART MARSHALL *Designer*
Somewhere round 1955/56 we were rehearsing a variety show where Ian Wallace was down to sing Gilbert and Sullivan's 'Tax Collector' song. As was customary, the secretary had typed the words of the song into the script for cutting and timing purposes and she'd placed a copy on top of the rather high desk I'd put in for Ian to stand at. The first time Ian went through the song, he happened to glance down, and up in the gallery where we were watching him in the monitor screens, we saw him suddenly burst into peals of laughter. While we were wondering what had happened he said, 'Take a look at the first two lines.'

They read:

> My stately pen is never lax
> When I am assessing income tax.

But in typing it, the secretary hadn't depressed the space-bar between 'pen' and 'is'.

BRIAN TESLER *Producer*
On one of the Dickie Henderson programmes, Shani Wallis was the guest star. It was when she was starring in *Call Me Madam*, so we didn't put her on till about twenty minutes after the start of the show because she

was coming straight from the Coliseum.

But when we started she hadn't even arrived yet, which was especially worrying because I'd built a chute that went from the back of the circle all the way down to the stage for her to slide down as a spectacular first entrance. When the time came for that and we'd still had no word that she'd got to us, Dickie just took a deep breath and announced, 'Ladies and gentlemen, Miss Shani Wallis'.

And, as luck would have it she'd turned up with so little time to spare, she hadn't bothered checking in. She just dashed up to the back-circle, hurled herself straight on to the chute and arrived on-stage dead on cue.

It was a hell of a thing to do, but there you are – with live shows you were dicing with danger all the time.

JOHN P. HAMILTON *Producer*

One of the shows Peter Sellers and Spike Milligan did for us had a sketch where Peter played Richard III. He was in the full gear, with a false nose and the Make-up Department had even managed to get the actual wig Olivier used at the Aldwych Theatre.

He did the 'Now is the winter of our discontent' bit, the entire thing in the grand Olivier style, then at the end of the speech – because this was during a period when he was having a terrible punch-up with the BBC for having come over to ITV – he declaimed, in the same Shakespearian voice, 'And can I do all this and yet not get a "Worker's Playtime"?'

JOAN KEMP-WELCH *Producer*

There was a big programme to celebrate the second anniversary of ITV. The first half was variety and the second half was drama, in the form of an Outside Broadcast from the Haymarket Theatre with people like Dame Edith Evans. I had the variety half, which they decided would be the life-story of Dickie Valentine. And what you must remember is that all this was before you could record and edit.

The number just prior to the first-half finale was Dickie and Albert Burdon doing the wallpaper-hanging sketch from their pantomime. The stage-staff had mixed the paste for them, but unfortunately they'd made it too thick, so that when they sloshed it on the wall and took a step back, whoops, they went for six. It was like a skating-rink; they had to clutch on to the tables to keep on their feet.

I immediately shouted to the Floor Manager, 'Quick, get the charge-hand to crawl in under the cameras – cameras, you stay waist-high – get him to crawl in and roll paper across the floor so they've got something to absorb the stuff.' So we then had the wonderful picture of scene-hands crawling all over the floor trying to roll the paper over this slithery stuff, while Dickie and Albert Burdon did their best to continue with the sketch. Then Reg, the charge-hand, fell into the big tub of paste, and there he was, lying on his back in it, legs and arms waving – the entire studio was in hysterics, and how Dickie and Albert Burdon got through to the end of that sketch I don't know.

But, needless to say, by the time they reached it we'd overrun by two minutes. So we never got to the big finale-scene, which was to have been Dickie sitting with Val Parnell in a stage-box watching Max Bygraves doing his act. But by the time we reached that, it was time to go to the Haymarket.

Still, I thought I'd done quite a good show, and when the telephone rang I answered it all prepared to receive congratulations. But it was John McMillan, who said, 'How dare you! How dare you cut that last item out!'

Well, I started to giggle, which only made things worse. 'I'm terribly sorry,' I said, 'but if you could have seen –'

'I don't want any excuses. Be in my office tomorrow morning at ten o'clock.'

I went up at ten the next morning, by which time he had heard the full story and Val Parnell had put in a good word, so he was a bit mollified. But only a bit.

BILL PODMORE *Cameraman*

I always wanted to do comedy. I remember losing one chance at it when I was up in front of a board for a director's job and Derek Grainger said to me, 'If I was a producer and I handed you a script for a comedy show that had only two laughs in it, what would you do?'

I said, 'Cut them and give it to the Drama Department.'

2 Drama

> You had those interval films – the potter's
> wheel and so on – and they rang a bell before
> the next act started, so that you could make the
> tea. It was sort of strangely civilised in
> those days, wasn't it?
> MICHAEL BOND *Cameraman*

That potter's wheel is probably early television's most indelible image. It was one of a batch of short films known as 'interludes' which the BBC used as a kind of non-commercial break whenever there was a hiatus between live programmes. The other interludes were equally soothing in their subject-matter – a kitten playing with a ball, a slowly turning windmill, a singularly placid waterfall – which made them particularly useful for bridging the intervals that were then mandatory between the acts of a television play. However, some Drama Department producers preferred devising their own form of *entr'acte* picture.

PADDY RUSSELL *Contract Stage Manager*
I have to stake a claim for being responsible for putting on the longest commercial ever to be seen on BBC TV during one of those intervals. It was in the early fifties, while we were doing a play called *Arrow To The Heart*, and in those early live days the interval was usually about five minutes. During it, directors – or producers, as they were called then – would often just put up a straightforward caption, the studio still being 'live'. But at other times, and I think Rudi Cartier started this, we used to show some sort of picture appropriate to the programme, such as props from the play.

Well, one of the key props in that particular production was a kind of satchel, a bag that had various bits and bobs in it, one of which was a jar of honey. All day I'd

Robert Harris and John van Eyssen in *Arrow To The Heart*

been saying to myself, 'I must get the label off that jar of honey', but it was a very busy show and I kept forgetting it. Then came the interval, and I was sculling around re-setting things when I happened to pass a monitor, took a look at what it was showing and nearly fainted. There was this jar of Gale's honey, straight-on to camera, right in the foreground. And that's how it stayed for five minutes! Five minutes! The first TV commercial in this country, and I suspect it's still one of the longest. I still don't understand why I didn't get a case of Gale's honey, though.

Paddy Russell also recalled another occupational hazard live drama could present in those days: the way that shortage of space sometimes obliged the production of a play to be spread across two studios. This provided particular problems for the Floor Manager, whose duty was to act as the producer's representative on earth; in other words, to receive instructions from the control gallery, via a set of earphones, and convey them to the technicians and actors down on the studio floor. With a two-studio production, that obviously entailed a fair amount of haring about, especially if, as was the case with Paddy, you were 'on the book': i.e., keeping a copy of the script at the ready in case an actor forgot his lines.

PADDY RUSSELL

The first two-studio drama at Alexandra Palace was Terence Rattigan's *Adventure Story*, with Andrew Osborn playing the lead and John Slater as Clitus, and we did it in Studios A and B.

There were no connecting doors between the two studios, so everyone had to use the doors into the corridor, which in both cases were at the far end of the studio. Although the play was written to give people time to get down there, some of the moves were a bit quick.

Besides being on the book, I was also playing the small part of a priestess, so I was in a wig and long robes, which I had got hooked up round my neck with a safety-pin so that at the end of every scene I could abandon whoever was performing and run like hell to the adjoining studio. We'd trained the prop boys to open the doors at the strategic moment so that we could make it out of there in time. Mercifully, none of the actors I left behind 'dried' – or, at least, if they did they got themselves out of it.

CHRISTINE HILLCOAT *Make-up Assistant*

I remember when they did *A Christmas Carol* at Alexandra Palace using the two studios linked by a long corridor. Everyone ran between them as fast as they could, but Bransby Williams, who was our Scrooge, and by then would have been in his eighties, didn't even walk very quickly. So the scene-hands made what I believe is called a 'fireman's lift' and he sat on their crossed hands chatting to them while they gave him a ride from one studio to the other. And when they put him down, he'd go straight into his acting as if he'd never moved.

Bransby Williams

SYBIL CAVE *Production Secretary*

Henry Oscar was in one of the two-studio Shakespeare productions – can't remember now which one – and instead of getting from Studio A to Studio B along the corridor, he decided to walk through the technical area because he was fascinated by the oscilloscopes and so on. Then he got chatting to the engineers and when the Floor Manager cued him for his entrance, he almost missed it – came rushing in and tried to run up a flight of perspective stairs, not the practical stairs.

COLIN CLEWES *Camera Tracker*

Of course, the perspective steps didn't bear his weight, so he went right through them and was left up to his knees in plaster. All I could do was just track in to show only the top half of him and that's how he delivered his speech – knee-deep in plaster stairs.

One of the most respected of the BBC's live drama offerings in those days was *Sunday Night Theatre*, and tales are still told about the number of viewers who used to change into evening-dress to watch it. It proved to be equally well remembered by those who had a hand in its productions, not least for the fact that every play it featured was given a live repeat later in the week.

ROSEMARY GILL *Production Secretary*
I remember the first time I was ever on a drama production. I went to work for Wolf Rilla and it was a thriller, set in a seaside place, and it was thought quite daring at the time because I think Wolf was one of those trendy-type guest producers. And, of course, it was live – the Sunday-night play. And this was the thing – it was repeated on the following Thursday. That gave you the feeling of working in a theatre, because you had the notices to look at, and if they were bad you still had to do it again on Thursday just the same. I don't think television has ever had that since.

HAL BURTON *Drama Director*
When I did my first television play – *Moonshine* by John Coates in 1953 – the umbilical cord between sound radio and television had not yet been broken and authors were still being paid by the minute, not by the play. We used to do the Sunday-night play live, then do it live again on the Thursday. By then, of course, the actors were more confident than they had been on the Sunday, so the cast used to get through the play much more quickly. Consequently, the author used to receive less money for the Thursday performance.

CYRIL WILKINS *Cameraman*
Pre-war, Royston Morley did a play called *The White*

Château and, to give it some realism, he had the local Territorial Army battery come up to Alexandra Palace that night.

Television guns scare Londoners

Daily Express Staff Reporter

NORTH LONDONERS heard heavy gunfire last night from the grounds of Alexandra Palace, rang up police stations in alarm, said old people and children were being "frightened out of their lives."

They were told the guns, two howitzers, were being fired by Territorials in connection with the televising of the wartime play, "The White Chateau."

The first alarm was at about 7.30. Each gun fired a trial shot. During the performance, between 9 and 9.30, about ten blank rounds were let off.

Terrified people telephoned the Daily Express. "Is it an air raid?" they asked. "Are we being attacked?"

They said their houses had shaken, that their children had awakened crying, and no warning of the firing had been given.

A B.B.C. official said: "There should have been no alarm. The programme had been fully advertised. It said the cast of 'The White Chateau' would have the co-operation of the 53rd (London) Medium Brigade R.A., T.A., and 7th (Middlesex) Regiment, T.A."

Daily Express 12 November 1938

ROYSTON MORLEY *Producer*

I had a camera on 1000 ft of cable out in the grounds and the battery set off about four 13-pounders. I was in the gallery of Studio B when that lot went off and the explosion was so enormous that I could hear the crashing of glass as quite a number of the windows of Ally Pally shattered. And the people of North London weren't too happy, either.

CYRIL WILKINS

It almost started a riot. Well, it was 1938, around Munich time, and when all those guns went off people came rushing out of their houses and started digging holes in their back gardens. The police had been warned, of course, but they hadn't realised it would cause a panic like that.

ROYSTON MORLEY

We apparently gave the impression that war had been declared. I can remember being on a bus next day and seeing a newspaper poster in Oxford Street that said 'BBC PRODUCER TERRIFIES NORTH LONDON'.

CYRIL WILKINS

Anyway, when it came to the question of repeating the play the following Thursday, the BBC said no guns, and that was that. Poor old Royston had to try and get these blokes to double back with fireworks, but this time a whole crowd from Wood Green and Muswell Hill had turned up to see the fun and when they saw that it was only fireworks they all started booing. Of course, that picked up on our microphones, so Royston had to cut back to the studio and that ruined the whole effect.

GEORGE CAMPEY *TV Publicity Officer*

Back in December 1954, when plays went out live on Sundays and were repeated on the following Thursday, I joined the BBC the Monday after their Sunday transmission of *1984*. That first day I was sent off to the country on some kind of brainwashing course to learn how the BBC worked, but while I was listening to the first lecture I was called out.

It was a phone-call from Lobby [S. J. de Lotbinière], who was then running the Programme Board, saying that he urgently wanted to consult with me. A car came for me and I was whisked back to Lime Grove for a meeting that had been called to consider whether or not *1984* should be put out again on Thursday. The main objection was that it was just before Christmas and that the scene showing the rats had caused a national outcry, both in the press and from people telephoning.

Lobby said, 'There's going to be a big public relations problem if we put it on again, so should we – or should we cancel the second showing?' I took a deep breath and said, 'I think we should go ahead with it.'

The Board was about fifty-fifty I think, so it was up to Lobby's casting vote and he decided to go ahead. In the event, there was no outcry on the following Thursday. Between the Sunday and Thursday, the story had spent itself, the outcry had died down, people had understood the rest of the play, and no one was fussy about it going out before Christmas. But I never did learn how the BBC worked.

'That scene showing the rats' ... However profound an impression it may have left on the viewing public – and there is evidence of a certain ageing cross-section who have slept with the landing light on ever since – its protagonists seem to have created almost the same amount of dissension behind the cameras. Once again, we have it on the authority of the lady who spent over ten years as Stage-cum-Floor Manager to Rudolph Cartier, the man who produced *1984*.

PADDY RUSSELL

Rudi insisted that we had genuine dyed-in-the-wool sewer rats. But we had to use such a hell of a lot of lighting in those days, because the cameras didn't have the clarity they have now, that when we got those rats into the studio they all passed out from the heat. So Jack

Rudolph Cartier and Sonia Dresdel

had to go down to the pet shop and get hold of whatever rats they had there.

JACK KINE *Visual Effects Designer*

They wanted the rats to go up the pipe and chew Peter Cushing's face. He was a marvellous actor but he didn't like rats. I didn't mind them. Anyway, all the pet shop had were white rats, so we brought a box of them back and I said to Bernie, 'How we going to make these brown?' and he said, 'We'll dye them.'

I said, 'We'll have the RSPCA after us. But we can make them up.'

I'll always remember that make-up. I said to

Christine [Hillcoat], 'Can I have a tube of Leichner Number 3?'

She said, 'What do you need it for? I do the make-up.' So I opened the box and said, 'Well, can you make these up?' And she disappeared, all knickers and stockings up the corridor. So we were the ones who covered the rats in Leichner Number 3.

'Bernie' is Bernard Wilkie who collaborated with Jack Kine in creating the department which eventually became known as 'Visual Effects'. In their time they were responsible for all manner of television wonders, from the Daleks in *Dr Who* to the various oddities on Michael Bentine's *It's a Square World*. Although Bernard and Jack were somewhat similar in appearance, Bernard was the more reserved and boffin-like in manner, as befitted one of the few men in the building who used to knit his own stair-carpet. *1984* was an important production for their department, and not solely because it was the first play whose author, Nigel Kneale, took the trouble to discuss with them beforehand the kind of special effects that might be included.

JACK KINE

1984 was our first ever official big-spend job on special effects. We had approximately £50. Even then we spent it as if the money was our own. We elected to go for ex-government surplus – like the eye, that thing that went round in each of the cells, those evil-looking cameras watching everything: they were gramophone motors with this revolving thing on the front. And old Bernard and me, we went rushing round the studio with a handle each, winding up those motors to keep them going, like the plates on a stick you see sometimes.

We also made the porn-write machine and at a touch of a button behind the scene we could make it judder and rock. I was in the wings watching Yvonne Mitchell doing her stuff and she suddenly screamed and her hand went into the machine. I came flying up and said, 'Are you all right?' and she said, 'Piss off, I'm acting.'

Peter Cushing and Yvonne
Mitchell in *1984*

PADDY RUSSELL *Floor Manager*

It was in *1984* that the key prop got whipped just before
transmission.

It was a little snowstorm paper-weight – one of those
you turn upside-down to watch the snow fall – and it was
used in a big scene between Winston and Julia where he
up-ends it, looks at the snow falling over the tiny village
and says, 'It's just like a little world.' Well, it disappeared
during the last dress-run or during the break – just
vanished totally out of the studio – and we couldn't get
another one because it was Sunday. Then Nigel Kneale,
who'd done the adaptation, remembered that he had one
like it at home. He didn't live in London – he was
somewhere out in the country – so his wife had to come
bolting up in a car with this wretched snowstorm. It
wasn't actually as good as the one we had because I don't
think there was a little village inside it, so in the end we
could only use it very discreetly.

Such emergencies were routine to anyone serving as Rudolph
Cartier's Floor Manager. A brilliant and flamboyant
Austrian, his predilection for large-scale productions was
matched by an almost total lack of regard for live television's
limitations. 'I'll need a hundred extras' was his customary
and immediate response to any new project – a foible which
lent relish to Frank Muir's remark on meeting him in a lift,

TO18159

'I understand your next play is *A Month In The Studio*.' And because Cartier's personal characteristics were as extravagant and action-filled as his shows, his control gallery to studio floor rows with Paddy became a long-running attraction.

PADDY RUSSELL

People used to come from all over the building to hear Rudi and me having one of our barneys. They were pure let-off of tension, and the interesting thing was that if anybody had asked Rudi or me afterwards what either of us had said and why we had the blow-up, neither of us would have been able to remember.

They began the first time I worked with him. That was on *Will Shakespeare*, with Peter Wyngarde playing the lead and John Schlesinger doing a walk-on. I had to mark out lines on the floor of the rehearsal room to show where the scenery would be in the studio, so I got to this dreadful little rehearsal room off the Holloway Road at some unearthly hour of the morning, but when I set about marking out the set, it wouldn't all go into this little room. So when Rudi arrived I explained to him the bits I had to leave out and we got on with the rehearsal. Then, some time later, we got to a scene where some musicians were supposed to pass behind a window, which was one of the bits of scenery I hadn't marked on the floor. And from the other end of the rehearsal room, he suddenly let off what I came to know as one of Rudi's typical eruptions.

Well – 'I'm not standing for this,' I thought, so I parked the script on the floor and said, 'Rudi, I told you about that this morning. If you want it all re-marked, you can re-mark it yourself,' and I walked out. I went down the road into this terrible little caff, thinking 'Well, that's the end of my BBC career,' but when I went to get myself a cup of tea I only had about fourpence in my pocket. So I had to go back to the rehearsal room to collect my bits and pieces, and as I was slipping quietly to where I had left my bag, Rudi said, 'Ah, Paddy – we are on page thirty-four', and before I knew it I had the script on my lap again. And ever after Rudi introduced me to everybody as 'my bad-tempered Irish Stage Manager'.

It was typical Rudi. He was marvellous. I did every production he did, until I became a director.

And those productions included *The Quatermass Experiment*, *Quatermass II* and *Quatermass and the Pit* – three 1950s serials which kept practically the entire population house-bound – as well as *Mother Courage*, *A Midsummer Night's Dream* and a succession of equally ambitious live operas.

The only other producer in that field whose name can still evoke the same quantity of delighted reminiscence is George More O'Ferrall, whose experience of television went back to 1936. That was when the BBC, with their traditional fond-ness for catchy titles, appointed him 'Senior Play Producer In Charge of Drama'. Subsequently, his production of *The Dark Lady of The Sonnets* was one of the programmes which re-opened the television service in 1946, and in the following year his *Hamlet* was awarded the television equivalent of an Oscar. He continued working till well into the sixties, but throughout that long and distinguished career – and this is perhaps what helps keep his memory so green – his grasp of the technological aspects of television production was never more than engagingly sketchy.

STEPHEN BUNDY *Designer*
In the very early days, when I asked George More O'Ferrall, 'How do you want this room designed?', he would say, 'I don't mind as long as you give me a few holes to get the actors on and off.'

On one play, there was one hole he was using as a door and it was actually a fireplace. I said, 'For God's sake, George, you can't bring people in and out through a fireplace.'

BIMBI HARRIS *Vision-mixer*
If anything ever went wrong when I was working in the control gallery with George More O'Ferrall, he would simply put his head down, almost in tears. Then, after

the show had been in progress a while longer, he would look up and say, 'Is it still going on?'

BILL WARD *Vision-mixer*

In 1938, I was in the control gallery when George More O'Ferrall did an adaptation of *Clive of India* where the author, W. P. Lipscombe, who was also a successful screen-writer, had written in a highly complicated 'montage' sequence. What this montage called for was a lot of fast and accurate cutting between four cameras in the studio and two film-outputs on telecine, one of them giving us various stock scenes of India – the Taj Mahal, Kashmir, all those places – while the other was a continuous loop of film showing just flames blazing and leaping. Down in the studio, we had one of the four cameras on a caption that had the word 'war' written on it in very large letters, the camera starting a long way back from it so that the word 'war' looked very tiny, then gradually tracking forward till 'WAR' was screaming at you. That same camera then had to be switched to captions showing illustrations of various wars – Crecy, The Black Hole, all that lot – while another of the cameras stayed on a kettle-drum that just kept going brrm ... brrm ... terrap. And throughout that, the remaining two cameras took shots of the actors who played the characters in the play ... Clive, the Indians, so on, all standing against a plain grey background.

And assuming all that came together at the right moment, what the montage would show would be a screen full of flames, then the word 'war' superimposed, gradually getting bigger as we tracked in; then, as that faded out, the face of Clive would come through, then Clive would fade out, in would come a shot of India, then – well, you can imagine the idea.

It was a long sequence, very long, went on for several minutes, which meant that everybody concerned – vision-mixer, sound-mixer, telecine operators, camera-men, Floor Manager – they were all depending on getting an enormous number of intricate split-second cues from the producer. Well, as you've probably heard, that sort of technical cueing wasn't exactly George More

O'Ferrall's strong point. And, sure enough, at the first rehearsal, the montage was pretty disastrous. So all of us technicians got together – I was the vision-mixer – and we said to George, 'Look, when we get to this sequence, all you do, George, is just say, "Cue montage" – and shut up.'

So that's how we rehearsed it, everybody in the gallery and down in the studio, and after a while we got it more or less right. More or less. But what could we do? We just had to take a chance. Came transmission time and we said to George, 'Don't forget now, George . . . "Cue montage", and then shut up.'

We came to the sequence, everybody's adrenalin flowing like mad . . . and George, good as his word, said, 'Cue montage', then sat back and simply watched. It worked like a dream. I mean it, it really did. Up came the flames, then 'war' came through, faded out, Clive's face came in, went out, India scenes, kettledrum, brrm . . . brrm . . . terrap. Everything! On and on it went. Beautiful! . . . And finally we came to the end of it, faded out, got on to the next scene – and George said, 'Oh, that was wonderful. Can we do it again?'

SYDNEY NEWMAN *Executive Producer*
I used George More O'Ferrall. He did some very classy work. He could draw big names from the film industry like Ann Todd, and other stalwarts of British stage and film.

Sydney Newman's approval placed the veteran O'Ferrall among the young lions who directed *Armchair Theatre* during the late fifties. That was the series of specially commissioned one-hour plays which freed television drama from its allegiance to stage adaptations and helped it become a force in its own right.

SYDNEY NEWMAN
The policy I adopted for *Armchair Theatre* was to do plays about contemporary Britain. No adaptations from

theatre or literary sources were wanted. The plays had to be fast and exciting and concerned with the turning points in contemporary society. It meant finding contemporary young British writers. We came up with people like Harold Pinter, Hugh Leonard, Clive Exton, Alun Owen, Angus Wilson ... many others. And by keeping the loyalties of directors like Philip Saville, Ted Kotcheff, Alan Cooke and Charles Jarrett it became a tight little team.

It was my job to assess the scripts and I would assign the directors. If I wanted a fast pace, exciting reality, I would choose Ted Kotcheff; for something sophisticated needing exotic camera work – that kind of thing, I'd pick Philip; for a solid highly polished job, I'd pick Charles Jarrett, and so on ...

VERITY LAMBERT *Production Assistant*
Of course there were the most monumental personality clashes. The main thing was that nobody – apart from Charles Jarrett, who went about his work rather quietly – nobody in the department really agreed with anybody else. There were some strong characters there and everybody had firm ideas about what they wanted to do and how they wanted to do it and nobody was afraid to speak up. Because it was such a small department, there would be wonderful moments like when, for example, Philip Saville wasn't happy about his script, or when Ted Kotcheff went over budget, and you would hear yells and screams coming from behind Sydney's closed door.

SYDNEY NEWMAN
No Trams to Lime Street, by Alun Owen, was the first play we did that really made TV history in Britain. It had a marvellous cast – Billie Whitelaw, Jack Hedley, Alfred Lynch and Tom Bell.

It took place in Liverpool. It went out on the air and the following day in my office at Teddington ten minutes after I read the rave reviews in the press, my phone rang. It was my managing director, Howard Thomas, who said, 'Sydney, will you please come over to my office right away?'

I figured, great, he's going to pat me on the back and say it was a lovely show last night. So I went over but Howard was looking somewhat glum. Seated next to him was his boss, the Group Managing Director of Associated British Picture Corporation, C. J. Latta, an American. I soon guessed that Latta had just torn a strip off him, because he couldn't understand 'the language talked last night'. Well, I being a Canadian and him being an American, I talk one side of the mouth and he speaks on the other side, so I said, 'C.J., they were talking with a Liverpool accent and, after all, we're North Americans. It might be tough for us, but everybody in Britain got it.'

'Don't give me that', he said. 'My chauffeur didn't understand it, and he's English. You tell those darn actors next time to speak fucking English.'

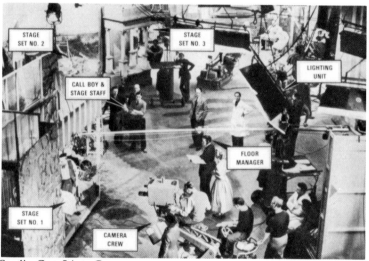

Studio G at Lime Grove

But despite the triumphs live drama managed to achieve – and in those days it could draw audiences larger than any other branch of television notched up – old drama-hands still hold that the most important skill it required was an above-average gift for taking emergency measures under unforeseen circumstances.

MICHAEL BOND *Cameraman*

Every day there was some kind of little disaster. I recall doing a Chekhov play where we'd got everything worked out in rehearsal and I had a mental image of what everybody looked like in the view-finder, then we went off for the tea-break and when we came back they all had a beard on. Didn't recognise anybody.

SHEELAGH REES *Production Secretary*

My first play was disastrous. It was *Cold Comfort Farm*, and it was at a time when we were all terribly busy and there was nobody to clear the copyright in advance. So when the producer said, 'Have we got the copyright?', I said, 'Well, I've sent the green form', went and investigated and found that, for copyright reasons, the play could not be televised. So there we were with the whole cast booked and nothing for them to perform. So the producer went along to French's, the big firm of play publishers, and found a play that had the same number of male and female actors and they all turned round and did that one. That was the first occasion that I wanted to die.

JANE SCRASE-DICKINS *Costume Designer*

One of the programmes I had when I first went to television in '55 was *Children of the New Forest*, a series of eight produced by Naomi Capon, and I don't think we had any filming at all in it. It was all done in the studio, with lots of fir-trees stuck into holders with sand round them. So as soon as I heard it was on, I went into Nathan's, the costume-hire people, and I said, 'How are you off for Roundheads?' – because they only kept so many of this sort of garment, and no way could the BBC afford to spend money making any extra ones. And they said, 'They're all in Spain on some film, but they should be back when you need them', which was all right except that because we were really very, very short of money, the few extras we were using had to play both Roundheads and Cavaliers.

This meant we dressed them basically as Roundheads, then we put a wig on them and a Cavalier's hat and a cloak, and they were Cavaliers. So what I did was put dressers behind bushes – and remember, this was to be a live show – and the extras charged through as Cavaliers, we changed them, and they rushed out the other side as Roundheads.

And after Naomi had made us do this for perfection over and over, everybody was terribly hot and dying for a cuppa, but still you had to go on rehearsing and re-hearsing because, this being live, the timing was crucial. Then there came a moment when I saw an enormous amount of shaking going on in one of the bushes, so I crept round to see what it was and we had a case of temperament going on. There was this marvellous dresser, Joe, a real character, and one of the extras was saying to him, 'I'm not changing any more, I'm just not. I've had it.' And Joe said, 'If Miss Dickins says you're going to be a Roundhead, you're going to be a bloody Roundhead.' And he picked up the pot helmet and shoved it down on the man's head. But what he hadn't done was remove the Cavalier wig ... I just convulsed and left them to it.

VERA SETON REID *Vision-mixer*
There was another production where the cast wore lace dresses which weren't available till just before transmis-sion. And the moment we went on the air, they all went completely transparent and all their titties showed. That was a great excitement.

PADDY RUSSELL *Floor Manager*
We did a live thriller, the name of which escapes me now, where the vital prop was a tiny document-camera – a Minox, which in those days was very new. It was featured in a two-handed scene where the character who had it was supposed to leave in a great hurry when a third character came in and interrupted them. In the event, the actor playing the part left in such a hurry he took the Minox with him instead of leaving it, as he should have done, in a cupboard where it was due to be found by the character who'd just entered. . .

When I saw what had happened I immediately went scrambling after him because, in those days of live transmission, when an actor had said his bit that was him finished for the day; he didn't need to hang around for re-takes. I grabbed him just as he was going through the studio door and I said, 'Give me the camera.' He didn't realise which one I meant for the moment, so I said, 'The Minox, you've still got it, give it to me.'

'Oh God, so I have.' He dug it out of his pocket and handed it over and I thought, 'Fine, that's that recovered.' So I shot back into the studio and then realised that the cupboard that the camera ought to have been stowed in was right at the back of the set. So I thought, the only thing I can do is go and place it there, otherwise the plot of the play will come to a grinding halt.

So I went into the set on my hands and knees, down between the actor and actress in there playing the scene. They looked a bit surprised as I came crawling between their feet but I got to the cupboard and edged it open. I stuffed the camera inside, closed the cupboard again – then realised that the two of them were heading towards me. So I had to stay on the floor in a rolled-up ball while they went through the whole scene of discovering the camera. I only managed to crawl out of the set when the action moved them away again.

They were pretty hairy days. You had to keep your wits about you.

DON GALE *Cameraman*

We had Margaret Lockwood's daughter doing a children's play, *Heidi*, in Studio H and how they got the set into that studio I don't know – we were really scraping the walls picture-wise to get a long shot. There was a new Floor Manager, Leonard somebody, and during rehearsals he'd painstakingly marked in his script every cue, every camera position, where every artist would be – it was his total bible that script, told him exactly what to do, where to go.

Well, the opening shot when we went on air was a wide shot of the whole set, so everybody in the studio was crammed up against the walls and Leonard held his script out to one side, while he was giving someone a cue with the other hand. They had live goats as part of the scenery and this goat near Leonard went 'crunch' and all he was left with was the top and the bottom of the script. From then on, I think viewers saw more shots of Leonard than they did of Heidi. The poor devil didn't know where he could stand, he was wandering around like a lost soul. But again, you see, it was 'live' – no way of stopping it.

VERA SETON-REID *Vision-mixer*

In 1949 we had Abraham Sofaer and Ernest Jay in an Irwin Shaw play called *The Gentle People*, most of which took place in a dinghy that was either moored alongside a landing-stage, or out in the middle of Sheepshead Bay.

(*left*) Abraham Sofaer and (*right*) Ernest Jay in *The Gentle People*

So James Bould, the designer, did something very experimental. He brought a huge tank into Studio A, and we used that as our set, with the actors in a flat-bottomed pram dinghy which kept capsizing.

Then suddenly, in the middle of the last run-through, we had a message to say 'Something's leaking through

Studio A's floor into the transmitter', which was on the floor underneath. Eric Fawcett, the producer, said to me, 'Do go down, dear, and check.'

So down I went and there was this old chap named Smith – he was known as 'Dusting and Maintenance' because he would say, 'There's always dusting and maintenance' – and there was old Smith sitting with an umbrella over him, and there were these enormous transmitter valves and he had boys holding umbrellas over all of them. And that's how the programme was transmitted.

Not that a transmitter failure would have been treated as a novelty by viewers of that era. In fact, the caption reading 'Normal service will be resumed as soon as possible' was used so frequently that the Drama Department had standard procedures for breakdowns. An off-screen presentation announcer would tell viewers what had happened, then a record would be played. That first record would always be something in keeping with the mood of the play, so it was generally music of a thoughtful or serious nature. If, by the time it had finished, matters showed no sign of improving, the announcer's microphone would be faded up again for a 'Well, I am afraid we are still unable to continue with the play' and, in the hope that the mood could still be maintained, there would be more suitably sedate music. If the fault had not been repaired when that record ended, then stage two had been reached.

To continue with serious music, it was held, might now plunge viewers into gloom and hostility. So after another consoling announcement, the next piece of music you heard would be of a distinctly jollier kind. If news was still bad, they deemed you had now had enough of that musically accompanied caption, so on would come an interlude. Should trouble persist to the point where even that might become intolerable, they would then put on a short 'interest' film, generally, as I recall, about Sweden.

When the play did get back on the air, the next decision that had to be made was, at what point should it re-start? Should it pick up from where it had left off? Or should it go back to a little while before that, so as to give viewers a chance to recall the plot and the actors a bit of time to warm up again? What often happened was a compromise: the actors would re-start the play a few seconds before resumption of service was announced, so that when the action was switched through to the viewers everybody was already in full spate.

Several of those we interviewed about that aspect of live drama claimed to have definite knowledge of somebody who was present on an occasion when the 'Normal service' caption appeared on the screen upside-down. We feel, however, that the following breakdown reports are somewhat more trust-worthy.

DON GALE *Cameraman*

When television was still only reaching the London area, you always had an off-air monitor from Alexandra Palace to tell you if the picture had died. In which case, you just used to stop and wait for them to repair the transmitter, then start again. And there was an occasion with one particular Floor Manager – I can remember exactly who he was: a very small man, very dapper in the way he dressed, Johnny Day – we used to call him 'Night and Day' – and it was a time when we weren't yet used to the fact that television had now got to the Midlands area, so there was more than one transmitter going. We were in the middle of a drama about King Charles – one would like to say it was the execution scene but I don't think so – it was leading up to something like that, though, something fairly heavy, and suddenly the picture in the gallery went. So the director told Johnny and he walked into shot and said, 'Hang on, hang on – the Palace is off the air' – which was rather good really, in a costume drama. So everybody wound down and the cameramen let all their cameras pan down to the floor, and we were almost starting to tell the dirty jokes when somebody said, 'Jesus Christ, what about Birmingham?'

ROYSTON MORLEY *Producer*

Prior to the war, around 1938, I did a Priestley play whose name I've forgotten but it was with Arthur

Sinclair and an actress who 'dried' while it was being transmitted. In those days the only thing you could do when that happened was to fade-out completely, then tell the actor the missing line. So I was just about to rush down to the studio when the gallery phone rang to say that because of a transmitter failure we'd been off the air for three minutes. So, to our immense relief, that 'dry' never went out.

CHRISTINE HILLCOAT *Make-up Assistant*
In the early days of live television, I once heard one elderly actor saying to another elderly actor, 'Don't worry, old boy. If you "dry", just carry on mouthing words. They'll think it's a technical fault and they've lost sound.'

While that advice could win an actor the gratitude of his fellows – Ian Wallace recalls hearing it from Harold Warrender, one of the suaver quiz-masters of the day – it also goes some way towards explaining why members of the production staff were occasionally less than starry-eyed about members of the acting profession.

BOB SERVICE *Cameraman*
In Associated-Rediffusion's early days, the studio discipline was fairly strict for technical people. You had to wear soft shoes in the studio, cameramen didn't speak unless it was something essential, you weren't allowed to sit on any furniture in the set, not even for a second, and there was certainly no smoking. But you got used to it, and we even got to the stage of playing practical jokes.

In *No Hiding Place*, or *Murder Bag* as it started off being called, Raymond Francis, who played the lead and had an enormous part to learn each week, used to hide cards with his lines on all over the set, as actors in live weekly dramas were sometimes obliged to do. And one day some wicked cameraman noticed he'd left a crib inside his desk drawer. He would just inch it open and glance down. Well, they took this bit of paper out while he was in Make-up and replaced it with a card saying 'You will dry now.' And, sure enough, he did.

(*left*) Raymond Francis and (*right*) Toke Townley in *No Hiding Place*

ELIZABETH AGOMBAR *Costume Designer*
> I remember once saying to Johnny Bradnock – Mrs Bradnock, she was a wonderful head of Make-up and Wardrobe, if you had any worries you went to her, and afterwards you came out thinking, 'What was I moaning about?' – and I can remember saying to her once, 'All this being psychological with actors and actresses.... Sometimes I'd like people to be psychological with me.'

MICHAEL BOND *Cameraman*
> I worked a lot on *Dixon of Dock Green*. Douglas Moodie was the producer, so I saw Jack Warner through his ageing process and watched Sergeant Flint write his lines out on the desk-sergeant's blotting-pad.

There was one live episode where I had a shot of Andy Crawford (Peter Byrne) reading a newspaper in the living-room and someone was supposed to come into the room, a girl. She didn't, and when Andy realised she wasn't going to, he simply kept on reading. The Floor Manager dashed back to the dressing-rooms – this was at Riverside Studios – and when he got there, he found this girl was having a bad attack of stage-fright. So he slapped her in the face, pulled her round, dragged her along the corridor into the studio, and shoved her through the door of the set. All the time I just stayed on the shot of Andy reading the paper. It seemed an age, but I spoke to people afterwards and they hadn't noticed at all.

DIANA PARRY *Production Assistant*
When we did *The Manor of Northstead*, with A. E. Matthews, who was famous for drying and forgetting to come on, we had a lovely Floor Manager, John Nicholson, who'd known Matty in the theatre, so he was actually on the show to look after Matty, walk him on at rehearsals and so on. Well, when we got to the live performance we came to a point where he was supposed to be on and he hadn't appeared. Lorraine Clewes, playing Bessie the maid, ad-libbed, 'Isn't his Lordship coming down to breakfast?', whereupon Marie Lohr with that lovely booming voice said, 'Oh, I do *hope* so.' John had now got Matty, so he pushed him on – better late than never – but next day one of the critics had the nerve to say it was a rather disorganised production. If only they'd realised …

The fact that they rarely did realise was not only true of live drama's involuntary stumbles. It could also be said of the amount of ingenuity that lay behind some of its more durable triumphs.

SYDNEY NEWMAN *Head of BBC Drama Group*
Dr Who was dreamed up when I moved to the BBC and

they asked me to fill a spot on Saturday afternoons which it was felt could get bigger audiences, between the fabulously rated sports coverage and an equally popular pop-music programme half an hour later. In the middle was a children's classic serial where the ratings dropped. The jump in appeal from sports to Charles Dickens was too great. If they moved the classic serial to Sunday afternoons, could I devise something that would maintain the ratings build? So I dreamed up *Dr Who*. It was a very simple idea about a senile old man of 720 years who was lost in outer space, and he had a space ship which was – well, on the style of an H. G. Wells time-space machine. He didn't know how to run it so that his passengers would never know where they would land up next in trying to get back to earth.

The thing had to have a very pedestrian everyday look to it but inside it was to be as vast as an airship. To handle the production I thought of Verity Lambert who'd been on my staff as a production assistant at ABC. I offered her the job as producer. She came on over. I handed her a sheet of paper with all my ideas for *Dr Who* on it, and one thing I was very clear about – 'No cheapjack bug-eyed monsters'.

VERITY LAMBERT *Producer*

So all I had to go on was this piece of paper he gave me, but on that one page was absolutely everything you needed to know. All the characters were there, including the Doctor; though I'd never have called him senile, more irascible and unpredictable. Childlike, perhaps.

The other thing that happened was that the first script that came in was all about cavemen, full of people saying 'Ug' and 'Ugghh'. And it's very difficult when you've been used to dealing with writers like Clive Exton to evaluate a script that consists mainly of grunts. What also made me nervous about the idea as a start to a serial was the danger of losing audiences if ape-like people are rushing round in hairy furs and things.

VIOLET MAITLAND *Dresser*

I was in at the beginning of *Dr Who* – William Hartnell,

wasn't it? – and I remember the first episode started in a sort of cave and there were all these old men lying around and their covering, in vital places, was mostly bits of fur. And, believe me, we had quite a job crawling round, Hilda was with me, making sure that all the fur was in the right places. Old gentlemen sometimes get fidgety.

VERITY LAMBERT

The second serial we got in was Terry Nation's Daleks. He was a comedy-writer who'd been commissioned by David Whittaker, our story-editor, and when I read the script through I thought it was wonderful – really exciting adventure stuff. There was a lot of political flak about it inside the BBC but the upshot was we went ahead with the Daleks and they were very successful. I went into Sydney's office after the start, rather full of myself, and instead of receiving all kinds of congratulations, there was this maddened figure saying, 'I told you, goddamit, no bug-eyed monsters!'

SYDNEY NEWMAN

I bawled the hell out of her. She said they weren't BEMs, but I wouldn't let her talk and she got angry. She said, 'Listen to me, will you listen to me? They are *not* bug-eyed monsters, they're human beings inside.' Then she told me there'd been an atomic holocaust and the only way they could get around was to be hermetically sealed inside that casing. And, ironically, the series became famous, as the world knows, because of the Daleks, the BEMs I never wanted.

JACK KINE *Visual Effects Designer*

I was uncle to those little buggers born out of poverty in Shepherd's Bush. Each one had an actor inside, sitting on a stool that had three castors, one at each side and one at the front – three-point suspension, always the best – with a little skirt round that hid everything. The actor sat wearing plimsolls, and it was like pushing yourself around on a typist's stool. Then, of course, you had the two arms, and there were the flashing lights which,

A Dalek, designed by Raymond Cusick, out and about in London

would you believe, were really the indicator lights off a Morris car, the old Morris Eight.

I remember looking at it and thinking, 'This'll never take off', but once one of the actors got inside, the things took on a life of their own. Mind you, in those early days, we'd never go for a tea-break without hearing a muffled cry and it would be some poor perisher who'd been left in his Dalek. He couldn't get the top off without someone helping him. What I think we did with the Daleks, although we never realised it, was make something that every child in the country could identify with. You just needed a cardboard box with cut-outs to put your arms through and any kid in the country could go round exterminating everything.

There were six of those original Daleks made, designed by Ray Cusick, the first one at TV Centre being put together by Bernard Wilkie, myself and Ray, the others done by a contractor out at Uxbridge who produced fibre-glass and wooden copies.

Today, of course, the Daleks are a bit like the bloke who had the same axe for sixty years. He had four new handles and six new heads, but it was the same axe he had for sixty years.

SYDNEY NEWMAN

After Verity really got going on the programme, a lot of well-meaning senior BBC officials started giving me a hard time at one of the regular Programme Review meetings, claiming that the series was frightening the hell out of kids every Saturday afternoon. I defended it, of course, saying that it wasn't terrifying – or if it was, not in a really psychologically hurtful way – but what really saved me from the onslaught of the other heads of departments was Huw Wheldon. He was chairing the meeting and he just burst out laughing. He said, 'I've got two kids at home – one four, one two – they're running around with wastepaper baskets over their heads yelling "Exterminate, exterminate!"' Everybody else laughed and the situation cooled down. Good old Huw.

The deeper our contributors delved into their memories of working in live drama, the more we found them marvelling at the sheer daring with which people escaped from being confined in a studio and tied to a budget.

GWEN FOYLE *Production Assistant*

When Don Taylor was a young producer, I worked with

him on one of the *Scotland Yard* episodes where we had one very fast scene, a scene that was all action and no words and had to go at a tremendous lick. Well, nowadays they'd get that effect by filming it, then putting speed into it by the way they edited it afterwards. But, of course, back in those days, Don didn't have that advantage. So he decided to give an impression of pace by doing something very unconventional – he got the actors to play the whole scene in slow-motion. That made it possible for him to take a lot of rapid shots of them from various angles, cutting very quickly from one to the other – cut, cut, cut – which made it look on the screen as though it was all happening very fast.

Well, the idea was so new and unorthodox, everybody had cold feet about it. In fact, on the first day of rehearsals the Technical Manager in the gallery issued him with a sort of official warning that because the show was live, the whole thing could very easily end in disaster. But Don said, 'It's my responsibility and I'd like to take the risk.'

So he did and it worked. By sheer chance, the show was recorded on 16mm for some reason or another, and afterwards all the crew asked if they could come and look at a playback. Don and I sat at the back while they watched it, and when it ended all those technicians turned round and stood up and applauded.

ROGER APPLETON *Engineer*
The series *No Hiding Place* was all live to begin with. We even used to do things like car chases inside the studio.

JAMES CELLAN-JONES *Producer*
There was a time in Scotland when we had no budget or facilities for filming scenes; absolutely everything had to be done live in the studio. But the technicians were so good, we were able to attempt some really high-class work, even major classic serials like Stendhal's *The Scarlet and the Black*.

That's got a large-scale melodramatic scene at the end where the girl brings her lover's head to be buried at night in this strange shrine in the mountains. How to do that in the studio and give it a great brooding outdoor feel?

Well, fortunately, the far end of that studio had a river outside, with a marvellous little Victorian bridge going across it. So we waited till it got dark, opened up the scenery-dock doors – huge double-doors up that end – and I had a great crowd of extras, all carrying flaming torches, walking in procession across the bridge into the studio and coming right up into close-up singing '*Dies Irae*'.

If, as Diana Parry and Rosemary Gill have indicated, one of the attractions of participating in a live TV play was the way its transmission could provide all the exhilaration of a theatrical first-night, it should also be remembered how that exhilaration sometimes went hand in hand with another familiar first-night emotion.

BERYL WATTS *Production Secretary*
The thing about 'live' was there always used to be a terrible feeling of anti-climax after the programme had gone out. You'd worked yourself into such a state, then suddenly, next day – slump.

SYBIL CAVE *Production Secretary*
I remember getting that awful let-down feeling after we did a French mediaeval mystery play from Bristol cathedral as an Outside Broadcast. We had all the seats taken out, there were 300 extras, the main camera was on tracks down the nave, we arranged for additional cameras from the Cardiff unit and we built our control room in the chapter house by off-loading the equipment in there and enclosing it all with tarpaulin like a tent. That led to some of the additional Red Cross people we had to bring in making remarks like 'Fancy those people watching it inside there when they could be in the cathedral and see it actually happening.'

But what with all the preparation and rehearsal, we worked on it so long that after it was over you got that awful deprived feeling. The play went out on Maundy Thursday, there was a huge party afterwards, then naturally people departed and you came down to earth with a bump.

I got home in time for early breakfast and I remember sitting there thinking, 'I didn't switch off the immersion heater in the cathedral school', which we had used for Make-up and dressing-rooms. And that made me feel sort of happy because it meant I could leave the house and get back to that environment again.

3 Outside Broadcasts

'We did an OB a day. Interesting OBs, like
cheese-making.'
DENIS FORMAN *OB Executive*

Cheese-making or Coronation, it was a time when anything
that appeared on our screens while it was actually taking place
somewhere else still smacked of the miraculous. That was
why live Outside Broadcasts could traipse so many of us
round a paper-plate factory, or take us behind the scenes at
a wholesale dry-cleaner's. OBs bestowed the new and privileged experience of being somewhere when you weren't
there, an advantage which played a major part in promoting
the sale of sets. It may also explain why, even to this day, OB
technicians and production staff tend to speak of their work
as the 'purest' form of television.

At that time, they divided their programmes into two categories: 'actuality' and 'built'. An actuality OB was one where
the cameras attended some public occasion not primarily
intended for television and over which they had no influence
– a circumstance difficult to envisage nowadays. Included in
that category would be such events as the Cup Final, a
symphony concert, or a royal occasion. A built OB, on the
other hand, meant something which the producer could to
some extent adjust or pre-plan for his own purposes, as with
the tour of a stately home, a visit to some fascinating per-
sonage, or cheese-making.

For the Outside Broadcast production team, however –
among whom, incidentally, the title of 'Floor Manager'
became, for some unfathomable OB reason, 'Stage Manager'
– both categories presented all the hazards implicit in the
word 'outside': weather, discomfort, and the attentions of
that section of the public they came to refer to as 'gapers'.

DEREK BURRELL-DAVIS *Producer*

They were having a round-up of what was going on all over the country at Easter – all live items – and we were down to do a piece from Bellevue, Manchester. Bellevue at that time was quite a good centre for entertainment. It had a Wall of Death, a zoo with performing sea-lions, an enormous Big Dipper and, of course, the thousands of people who'd be there.

So we rehearsed a nice little fifteen-minute piece for our part of the programme and I employed a very good little Northern actor, Herbert Smith, to be principal commentator and, as the subsidiary commentator, a man called Fred Fairclough. We were going to start by the Big Dipper, then go over to the sea-lion pool, then we were going to see this excellent Wall of Death act they had, which was a man called Speedy Something, with his blonde Amazon partner. They were going to do incredible things on a motor-bike, then we were coming back to Fred, who'd be eating fish and chips, wearing a flat hat and scarf like they did then, he would do our goodbyes, and that would be our bit showing Easter Monday in the North.

We had a very nice rehearsal; then – as we broke for a short time to check cameras before the live transmission – down it came. We had a monsoon-type downpour, an incredible downpour – it came down solid. And, because it had been such a lovely hot day, everything started steaming. So instead of the thousands of people, we had acres and acres of empty asphalt with the steam rising off it. I'd hoped that the rain wouldn't stop, because at least viewers would then see what had happened.

Anyway, my Stage Manager rounded up a few people and said to Herbert Smith, 'Get up on the Big Dipper', but as he touched it, he got an electric shock. What had happened was that, due to the rain, together with our lights or cable or something, every part of it was now live – we couldn't use it.

But now we were on air. Herbert gave the opening welcome and as he couldn't do anything with the Big

Dipper now, he handed over to Fred Fairclough at the sea lion pool, where I had another camera waiting. All I had in those days were three cameras.

But as I cut to the second one, it went into what's known as 'reverse phase' – all the blacks went white – so what we saw was a lot of white sea lions swimming about in a black pool. We obviously couldn't stay with that so I said, 'Camera Three, I'm coming to you.'

'Don't come to me,' Camera Three said, 'I'm only halfway to where I'm supposed to be.'

I said, 'Never mind that, I haven't got another camera to go to.' So I went to Three and, sure enough, he was doing an extraordinarily bumpy 'track' to where he'd been expecting me to join him in ten or twelve minutes' time, at the Wall of Death. Only when he got there now, there was Speedy – I remember now, they were Australians – there was this scene of Speedy lying back on a bench with his boots off drinking beer, while his blonde Amazon partner was changing her sweater. (With her back to camera, fortunately.) Both of them looked round, horrified.

Well, I couldn't stay with that scene either, so I handed back to my opening commentator, who ad-libbed something on the lines of, 'Well, we've had a bit of a downpour here, but that's life in Manchester.' I kept the camera on him eating his fish and chips, because that was the only bit of the script that had worked, and I think I kept on the air about four minutes out of the fifteen-minute item.

Next day, a Manchester newspaper said, 'We don't know who this new young London producer is, but if that's the way he's going to portray what life's like in the North, the sooner he goes home the better.' It went on to say, 'We do not wear flat hats, we certainly don't eat fish and chips out of newspapers.' Made no allowances at all.

JOHN LANE *Stage Manager*

One of the very first OBs for *Play School* was at the zoo. Michael Grafton Robinson was in the control van directing a sequence where I was stuck way over in another region of the zoo. That meant the only way I

Calais *en fête*: Richard Dimbleby commentating during the first cross-channel OB

could communicate with him during rehearsal was by speaking into the microphone that Carole Ward, our presenter, had concealed down her cleavage. So every time I received an instruction through my earphones I'd acknowledge it by going over to Carole and saying into her mike, 'Yes, Michael, fine, you'd like it over there a bit further, Michael? All right, Michael' – then I'd go away and do it.

After about half an hour of this, something cropped up I wasn't sure about, so I bent over Carole's chest again and said, 'Michael, can I query something?' Whereupon a member of the public who'd been nearby watching piped up and said, 'Here, mate, why don't you try talking to Charlie on the other side for a change?'

SYLVIA PETERS *Presenter*
My first OB was from London airport with Charles Gardner, the BBC Air Correspondent. I didn't even know what an OB was, but they had a helicopter with a rope-ladder I was supposed to climb up to get inside

and they'd sent me there on an airport coach so that I could interview all the people going to the airport. I was only twenty at the time, no experience of reporting, and it turned out that all these people were going on dirty weekends and none of them wanted to be interviewed. So I started to talk about what you could get at the duty-free and I showed so many labels saying 'Gordon's Gin' that I nearly got the sack afterwards. And that awful helicopter – nobody had thought about the wind blowing up my skirt as I tried to climb the rope-ladder.

JOHN SUMMERS *Cameraman*
In the late forties, early fifties, they had these programmes from Alexandra Palace that were OBs in the sense that we'd put a long lead on a camera and take it outside the studio into the Palace grounds. They did it a lot for afternoon programmes and, often as not, you got no rehearsal and sometimes you didn't even know what the programme was going to be about. You just hauled your camera out there, went on the air live and did whatever your director said.

One programme of that kind which I particularly remember was a bee-keeper showing viewers how to hive off bees. Out came a skip of wild bees on to a table – thousands of wild bees, I could feel them on my hands. So I stuck my head a bit tighter into the view-finder and I heard the director's voice in my earphones, 'In you go, Camera One. Let's fill the screen with bees.'

While I was still considering that, I heard the bee-expert explain, 'First of all, you must pick out the queen bee.'

Straight away the director chimes in. 'What are you waiting for, Camera One? In you go on the queen.'

I looked round for my tracker to push my camera forward but he'd gone. Probably a while back. I can remember doing the rest of that programme with the camera covered in bees, my hands covered in bees, bees all over my head. But I didn't get stung.

ANDREW MILLER-JONES *Producer*
I used to do a lot of what were called 'local' Outside

Broadcasts. These were programmes that were produced in the studio, but the cameras were outside in the grounds of Alexandra Palace, linked to the studio by cables that ran through a culvert under the road.

The Women's League of Health and Beauty during a local OB from Alexandra Palace

We did things like showing people how to keep bees and we had our own beehive out there. On one occasion we were demonstrating how to centrifuge the honey out of the combs and when we were shown the stuff inside it was all bright red. This was because the lazy bees, instead of gathering nectar from flowers and things, had just gone down the road and got all their sugar from the waste-products of Batgers' confectionery factory.

CHRISTINE HILLCOAT *Make-up Assistant*
There were local OBs with Fred Streeter, who did a gardening programme. Dear old Fred Streeter and his garden – I believe only the willow tree is left now. He

always used to have apples and things in his pockets and after he was made up he'd always produce an apple out of his pocket for you, which made you feel about fifteen.

Fred Streeter in the television garden at Alexandra Palace, 1946

DENIS FORMAN *OB Executive*

At Granada we were short of transmission hours and one way of filling them was by very long OBs. Some of them turned out to be real headaches, like the one we'd planned to do about cycling with Reg Harris, the champion cyclist. He broke his wheel or something, so we were obliged to do an entire programme showing him just standing in the stadium talking. For a whole hour.

MIKE SCOTT *Stage Manager*

I well remember a live OB from Fleetwood, the grand finale of which involved launching a lifeboat. As the programme's Stage Manager it was my job to stand in the lifeboat house and cue the cox to smite the heavy blow with a sledgehammer that would remove the cleave-pin holding the lifeboat on its ramp and send that forty tons of lifeboat thundering down into the sea.

To this day I am totally convinced – and the director remains totally unconvinced – that he said, 'Cue the lifeboat.' Anyway, I did cue it and as the forty tons did indeed start hurtling its way down to the sea I heard the director's voice in my earphones saying, 'Too soon, too soon – bring it back.'

DENIS FORMAN *OB Executive*

Yet another harrowing hour was the OB from a gypsy encampment, where we'd announced our intention of interviewing these interesting gypsies about their simple, outdoor lifestyle. Just before we went on the air, those gypsies all got into their saloon-cars and drove away. Not a gypsy left in sight. The only person still around was a gypsy expert who'd turned up from Chester or somewhere. So we spent the entire hour interviewing him.

ALAN MOUNCER *Cameraman*

An OB I remember in 1951 was from a ski jump on Hampstead Heath. They imported the snow and it melted.

SYBIL HARPER *Producer's Assistant*

Different OBs called for different abilities. For something like the Royal Tournament, for instance, you and your producer would go along and watch several performances beforehand, to familiarise yourself with what was going to happen and how it would happen and when and where. In that case, drawing was a useful accomplishment, so as to have a diagram of what went on in, say, a musical ride, or to show in what order motorcyclists criss-crossed with each other.

You sat in the semi-darkness and made notes of which end or side of the arena the various items entered from, which way they proceeded and where they made an exit. These enabled a director to work out his camera-script, from which the cameramen could be given camera cards to work from.

In this respect that kind of OB was different from a

sports event, such as boxing, where more or less everything had to be done off the cuff.

TINY DURHAM *Sound Engineer*
Around 1953, we were doing a boxing OB from somewhere in Scotland, probably St Andrew's Hall, and my
technical assistant was Cecil Hawthorne. As usual, he
slung our effects-microphone above the centre of the
ring, but it turned out to be one of those fights where the
boxers always seem to be in one corner or another. So
Cecil said to both of them, 'Please try and box under the
microphone.'

DON GALE *Cameraman*
Soon after ITV arrived on the air, they transmitted a
boxing-match where the last shot before the commercial
break showed one of the boxers drinking from a bottle.
This was followed immediately by an advert for somebody's beer. When they cut back to the boxing the same
boxer was leaning over the ropes spitting out into a
bucket.

BINNIE MARCUS *Producer's Assistant*
It was a quiet spell during a cricket OB, one of those
times when the camera wanders round the field looking
for pictures and the commentators have to find something to say. The camera stopped at a little refreshment
booth where there were a couple of men drinking, and
Denis Compton said, 'That looks nice. A nice refreshing
drink of Coke.'
  Everyone in the control van gasped, and when we
arrived next morning there waiting for us were two
enormous crates of Coca Cola.

IAN ORR-EWING *OB Assistant*
We would have liked to televise greyhound-racing in the
early days, but we were inhibited by Sir John Reith's
dictum – and I think this applied to sound radio, too –
that it was undesirable to give it any publicity because,
with unemployment high and poverty high, it might
encourage poor people to bet on greyhounds. So not

only were we not allowed to go to the White City but
even at horse races you had to make sure not to place an
effects-microphone anywhere near the bookmakers.
They once actually made me withdraw a microphone
because they could hear a bookie shouting 'Three to one
the favourite'.

SYBIL HARPER *Producer's Assistant*
My very first programme when I went to OBs was horse
racing and the next one was *Come Dancing*. No one told
me what I had to do on that, probably because in those
days you were supposed to know what was required of
you by some kind of instinct. I'd learnt from my training
about timing each item and making a note of the music
for performing rights returns, but apart from that all I
had to draw on was what I'd picked up from doing
racing. There, part of the PA's job had been to make sure
that every horse in the paddock appeared on screen,
because viewers sometimes only placed a bet after seeing
what a horse looked like. It was something I hadn't
found difficult because each horse had a number on it
you could simply check off as it came on screen.

Then it occurred to me that the dancers were also
wearing numbers and that *Come Dancing* was also a
competitive event. So I simply treated the dancers as
though they were horses. Just as well, too, because my
director, Denis Monger, suddenly turned to me and
said, 'Which couples haven't we seen?'

MARY KEENE *Producer's Assistant*
Every year we used to do an OB from the Earl's Court
Radio Show, and on one occasion there'd been an item
on Scottish sports, particularly tossing the caber. We'd
finished it, and some of us were still around working out
arrangements for the next day's show when we had our
attention drawn to the arena. There in the middle of it
was Harry Secombe. We'd heard he'd been appearing in
another part of Earl's Court – but now here he was,
centre-arena, staggering and careering about with an
enormous caber. Well, of course we were alarmed, not
just for him but because of all the cameras and expensive

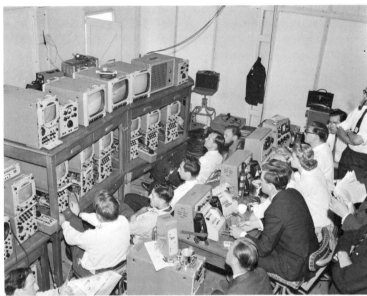

The control room at the first ITV OB from Wimbledon, 1957 (*below*) The miles of cable behind the camera control equipment

equipment around. He started shouting and pleading for help, but we didn't know how to help a man holding a caber, so we just stood there holding our breath and waiting for the crash.

Finally, he managed to throw it, and there wasn't any crash, just a plop. The caber was one he'd made up himself, out of papier mâché.

DEREK BURRELL-DAVIS *Producer*
Just before Christmas one year, we had to do a *Saturday Night Out* showing some troops departing from Harwich to serve in Germany. They were to be shown getting off the train and marching on to the ship, and as it was all going to be live, everything had to be planned very carefully. But I'd got an undertaking from British Rail that the train would be on time, the War Office had been sorted out and we'd been promised that a detachment of Guards would be clued up and ready.

It all started off beautifully. The train was not only on time, it was early and standing by for its cue. I was working with a new Stage Manager who'd recently come down from the North and had been pushed to me for training; a very likely lad, a bit reserved at that time, called Bryan Cowgill. I told him to cue the train in. He cued it. Into the station it steamed, out on to the platform jumped the soldiers, and I waited for the Guards detachment to start marching off. But they didn't. And there was the most appalling hiatus.

I don't suppose it was actually more than half a minute or so, but you know what these things are like when you're directing – it seemed like half an hour. At the time I had no idea what had happened, but what I found out afterwards was that Cowgill had jumped aboard for a final check and a Guards sergeant had told him there was a Guards major along who'd insisted on taking command.

'Okay,' Cowgill said, 'let me talk to him.' And when he'd explained, the major said, 'These troops will march off when I give the command, not you television wallahs.'

Cowgill said, 'But the War Office –'

'I don't care what little schemes you've arranged, I'm the senior officer here and they don't move till I say so.'

So there was the major striding up and down his line of troops, tapping his boots with his cane and so on, and being all masterful. Then suddenly out of the gloom came a figure wearing an Army greatcoat and beret whose voice rang out, 'Coldstream Guards, attention! Right turn, quick march!'

They marched off, leaving the major absolutely fuming. It was, of course, Bryan showing why he got to be the top executive he later became. So the programme got under way again and it was quite a success. In fact the major earned a reprimand. The only thing was, I wonder who told those soldiers to stop.

DOUGLAS HESPE *Stage Manager*

I was on a programme, *This Is Your RAF*, and its opening shot was the take-off of six Javelins, very fast aircraft with a take-off speed of about 250 knots in 12 seconds. For some strange reason it was decided that their cue for taking-off wouldn't come over the radio but from the programme's Stage Manager – which was me. This was despite the fact that the only place where all six of the pilots would be able to see me out of their small windscreens was if I stood right in the middle of the runway.

So, after signing all sorts of irresponsibility chits, I was given special permission to stand there, right in their path, and cue them by dropping a handkerchief. And so that I could hear my own instructions from Denis Monger, the producer, over the noise the Javelins made – which was above pain level – the engineers had to put some special equipment in my earphones to amplify his voice. The consequence was, Denis only had to cough and I thought my head was being blown off.

When the moment came, I raised my handkerchief, dropped it, those six planes came hurtling at me, I dived away but I can't tell you how near they came to running me down. It was the nearest I've ever been to a take-off. The RAF obviously thought the BBC, in allowing people to do things like that, was plain nutty.

DEREK BURRELL-DAVIS *Producer*

I'll never forget a programme I did from Manchester docks in 1952 with an OB unit. I directed – 'produced' as we said then – and Johnny Vernon was the Stage Manager. The first part went well, but then I got myself in a knot from trying to do too much – 'the great documentary producer'. We'd released a load of cats to get arty shots of them walking over wet cobbles, we'd cued the night-shift to come clattering in, and we'd had cameras aboard ships, lowering them down the holds and so on. Now we were approaching the pay-off for the programme, which I'd decided would be a goodnight from all the ships in the harbour by having them all sound their hooters at the same time.

I don't quite know what happened – perhaps Johnny got his cue muddled or something – but with about six minutes still to go, all those ships, the whole eight of them, let off their sirens simultaneously. The bloke on sound wasn't ready for it, I wasn't ready for it, so viewers found their whole television picture suddenly rolling and juddering, while I thought, 'That's done it. Pay-off to programme six or seven minutes too soon – what can I do now?'

But unexpected help arrived. The Manchester fire brigade, hearing this incredible noise, came tearing on to the docks in full force to see what needed putting out. And their dramatic arrival gave me some smashing closing pictures.

BILL WARD *Sound Engineer*

We were covering a pre-war Boat Race one Saturday afternoon – I think this must have been 1939 – and I was on duty at Alexandra Palace as sound-mixer.

Now when we did the Boat Race in those days we didn't have enough Outside Broadcast mobile units to follow the boats the full length of the course, so we only showed the start and the finish on camera. After the start, we came back into the studio, where we followed the race by maps and diagrams, then when the boats came in sight of our camera at the finish we went back to the OB unit.

Cameraman
Steve Wade
and Stage
Manager Ian
Orr-Ewing

(*below*)
Reporting a
Common-
wealth leaders'
meeting at
Downing
Street

What happened on this occasion, though, was that just before we went on the air, someone repairing the road outside Alexandra Palace put a pick or a pneumatic drill through the sound cable. So although we had a picture, we completely lost all sound. I had no sound-contact of any kind with anyone in the outside world, because this chap out in the road had gone through every circuit including the telephone. So we were completely isolated.

What I suddenly remembered, though, was that downstairs in the lines-termination room we had a quality wireless receiver. So, knowing that John Snagge was giving a sound commentary for the whole of the Boat Race on Daventry 5XX Long Wave, I went down and plugged in that emergency receiver and put that up on my sound bank. We then conducted the whole thing without any contact with the outside world at all. The announcer in the studio simply did what he could to match John Snagge's wireless commentary to the studio diagrams and maps and to whatever OB pictures we got from outside.

We did the whole race, and I honestly don't believe anyone watching realised there was anything amiss.

Coincidentally, there was a reversal of those roles during the 1952 Boat Race. The BBC sound-launch broke down, leaving John Snagge drifting further and further behind the two crews, so the radio sound-circuit was swiftly switched into the television sound-circuit. Michael Henderson then saved the situation by delivering an ingenious sound-and-vision commentary for both viewers and listeners.

But the hero of the 1939 occasion, who went on to become one of the world's most experienced all-round TV craftsmen, can lay claim to another rare distinction in the OB field.

BILL WARD *Sound Assistant*

I was on the first Outside Broadcast in 1937. The first Outside Broadcast of all time. The Coronation of King George VI, and I was right in the middle of the Apsley

Gate. I didn't have any particular feelings of it as a historic event, though, because everything those days was pioneering. We were making history all the time.

In terms of making history, however, it was the 1953 Coronation, the one starring Queen Elizabeth, that finally brought television-watching a measure of respectability. But while much has been said about the spectacular rise in viewing figures achieved as a result of that one live OB, less has been heard about the new status it conferred on those who worked in the medium.

ROS POOL *Secretary*
I joined the BBC secretarial reserve in 1947 as a short-hand typist and when the establishment at Broadcasting House found out I was living with a cousin in Muswell Hill at the time, they said would I go to Alexandra Palace? 'It's this television,' they said. 'We can't get people to go all the way up there, they don't think there's any future in it. It's like going to one of the Regions.'

DON GALE *Cameraman*
When I went into television from sound, I had to go to my senior engineer to ask for the transfer. And he said, did I realise I was putting my career in jeopardy because television was only a passing fad – it would never catch on?

ROYSTON MORLEY *Producer*
Actors in television plays were paid two-thirds of what they would have got for appearing on radio. The logic of this was based on the smallness of the TV audience as compared with the radio audience at that time.

MAGGIE SAUNDERS *Assistant Floor Manager*
It wasn't till after the Coronation that you suddenly heard people saying, 'Did you see such and such on TV?' Before then it had never been a topic of conversation. But the Coronation did it. That and the Boat Race.

Although all the untold behind-the-camera stories about that historic Coronation OB now appear to have been told in front of the camera, our interviewees managed to come up with a few untapped reminiscences.

GEORGE CAMPEY Evening Standard *Television Correspondent*
There was a whole question-mark over whether the Coronation would be televised at all, because Churchill and the establishment were against it. The TV people talked Churchill round, but even then it was by no means sure. I was keeping a close eye on developments, writing 'will-it, won't-it' stories, my guess being that it would. Then one day I was sitting in my office before lunch and my telephone rang. A muffled voice, obviously speaking with a handkerchief over the mouthpiece said, 'If you come down to the Abbey, you will see something of interest to you.' I went haring off down there in a taxi and when I got to the Abbey I found the Duke of Norfolk and Peter Dimmock, then Assistant Head of Outside Broadcasts, going round selecting places for cameras. I knew I had a scoop.

PETER DIMMOCK *Producer*
The establishment were very much against cameras in the Abbey and there was a rule saying the camera couldn't be nearer to the Queen than 30 feet. So I took a camera into the Abbey to demonstrate and I put a 2-inch lens into it, placed the camera 30 feet away and showed them, 'Look – marvellous.' What they didn't know, and what I knew, was that on the day I'd use a 12-inch lens and I'd get the Queen in close-up.

DEREK BURRELL-DAVIS *Producer*
We were gathered in from all parts of the compass to take part in the Coronation and I was given Grosvenor Gate, Hyde Park. That's where we got what I still believe was the best shot of Queen Salote of Tonga. It was raining, but Queen Salote had chosen to leave the hood of her

The Coronation
(*below*) Peter Dimmock in the control room at Westminster Abbey

carriage down. So I suddenly had an idea. I said to my Stage Manager, Willie Cave, 'Go out there on the platform and wave at her. Or better still, do a deep bow.'

So he climbed on to the camera platform and as she went by he gave her a deep bow – and she got up in her carriage and bowed directly back to him. Which meant, of course, directly to the camera. It made a most extraordinary shot.

DOUGLAS HESPE *Producer*

I had three cameras stationed about a hundred yards down the Mall from Admiralty Arch and, like all the other directors on the route, I was searching for some vivid pictures to offer my master director who was in charge of what got transmitted.

I asked one of the cameras if he had anything interesting to show me, and when he focused on one of the guardsmen lining the route, I said, 'Show me his face ... Now pan down to his tunic ... His belt ... Now let me have a look at his boots' – and when that camera got down to them, I saw what must have been the most highly polished pair of boots in the British Army. So highly polished that I asked for a close-up of just one toe-cap and there, reflected in it, you could plainly see all the guardsmen lining the road alongside him up to Admiralty Arch and in the background, a perfect picture of the Arch itself. All framed inside that one gleaming toecap!

Very excited, I got on to my master director, explained what I had, and he said, 'Okay, Admiralty Arch, I'll come to your boot in two minutes.' Then I heard him explaining to the commentator what I had and when he'd get to it. Then, through my earphones I got, 'Coming to your boot in one minute, Admiralty Arch,' ... 'Coming to your boot in 30 seconds' ... 'In 10 seconds' – then, 'Admiralty Arch, coming to your boot now!'

And, as the words left his mouth, I heard a voice shout, 'Two paces forward, MARCH!'

PETER DIMMOCK *Producer*

On the preamble sequence in the Abbey we were doing the ambassadors, with Richard Dimbleby naming them all, and when he was still halfway through, Princess Margaret's procession came into view about a minute early.

Now this shows how marvellous Richard was in those early days of television. The ambassador we had the camera on happened to stand up just as I screamed into Richard's headphones, 'Richard, Princess Margaret's procession's coming under the choir screen!' And without a moment's pause, Richard said, 'And now he stands, as well he might, to greet Princess Margaret's procession' – so allowing me to pan the camera straight over. He was so quick, so adroit – a dream to work with.

TINY DURHAM *Sound Engineer*

One of the ancillary events I covered was the display of Coronation dresses at St James's Palace, with Richard Dimbleby as commentator. The Queen Mother came to see them and when she paused to talk with Richard we lost sound. It all went strangely muffled for a while and we couldn't think why or how it had happened.

Then, later, Richard told me, 'When the Queen Mum came up, she started to compliment me on my Coronation commentary. And as that kind of personal chat from royalty isn't supposed to go out on the air, I slipped the mike up my coat-tails.'

PETER DIMMOCK

Something I've never forgotten about the Coronation is that about six-thirty in the morning I went down to the control room we'd built outside the Henry VIII Chapel and noticed that just nearby were the peers' loos. Well, thinking I might as well make use of them I went inside, and I could not believe my eyes. They'd put purple velvet on all the seats! All those Elsans, a row of ordinary Elsans, but – could you imagine? – in 1953, because the loos were to be used by peers, they had to have purple velvet lavatory seats. The only time in my life I've sat on a deep purple lavatory seat. Very comfortable it was, too.

Such privileged glimpses of the underside of solemn ceremonial were counted as one of the perks of working in OB
departments, which could always rely on being conscripted
for events of national or historic significance. But if the
trumpet of history was ever sounding at their ear, no-one we
spoke to seemed to have been deafened by it.

IAN ORR-EWING *OB Assistant*
Most people have seen that famous newsreel scene of
Neville Chamberlain getting out of the aeroplane after
coming back from his meeting with Hitler in 1938 – you
must know it, the one where he waves the piece of paper
– but what's less well known is that the scene was also
televised live as an OB. I found out that he was due to
land at four o'clock at Heston airport – or aerodrome, as
it was called then – so, the day before, I checked to see
if one of the two OB vehicles was available in the garage
at base and there was an OB van free and I got permission to take it to Heston.

KEITH EDELSTEN *Engineer*
In September 1938 we were hanging about at the back
of Alexandra Palace, doing maintenance, and we were
suddenly told, 'Right, all of you, get to Heston airport.'
So we went out there, got the cameras on to the roof,
and the aeroplane came in. I held the microphone, and
this funny old man came out waving a piece of paper:
'Peace in our time'. There was a big film cameraman
from the newsreel who said, 'Silly old bastard.' These
history things are very interesting.

LEONARD MIALL *Head of TV Talks*
We televised the first live OB from a Labour Party
conference in 1955. At the end of proceedings on the
first day – the Monday – that year's chairman, Dr Edith
Summerskill, announced that the television cameras
would be present the following morning and warned the
delegates that the lights would probably be intolerable.

Next morning Dr Summerskill was there in dark glasses and a wide-brimmed hat. Most of the others on the platform were similarly protected. They looked rather like stereotype Chicago gangsters.

What none of them knew was the lighting supervisor – a splendid character known as 'Grump' Mayhew – had had all the television lights switched on throughout Monday's proceedings to test out the cameras. So there was some surprise, and later chagrin, when the first debate started on Tuesday morning and the lighting was discovered to be no worse than the day before.

'Grump' was the nickname for an engineer who was, of course, far from grumpy. When he went to Sandringham in 1957 to light the Queen's Christmas broadcast on television, she heard the other members of the crew calling him by his nickname and, wishing to ask him something, she courteously addressed him as 'Mr Grump'.

ALAN MOUNCER *Cameraman*

The only royal Christmas Day broadcast that was done live from Sandringham was in 1957. BBC Catering sent out a full Christmas lunch in hampers which we ate before the broadcast in the scouts' hut on the Sandringham estate. And while we were in the middle of it, the lady herself came in and wished us a happy Christmas. We stood up and gave the best loyal toast there's ever been with the main participant present. Television being such a new thing in those days, every member of the royal family had visited us at some time or another during the previous three days we'd been there preparing. I didn't recognise the Queen Mother because I'd never seen her without either a hat or a tiara.

TINY DURHAM *Sound Engineer*

When we covered the launching of the royal yacht *Britannia*, I was on sound control. We came to the point where Her Majesty was going to press the button and say a few words to launch the ship and I found myself in a bit of a quandary. When exactly should I fade up sound on her microphone? If I did it too early I might just catch her saying something like 'Is my hat on straight?' A fraction late and I might miss her official words. Sitting there in the control van, it was difficult to tell: she couldn't give me a cue, and I certainly couldn't send her a message saying, 'All right, Your Majesty, you can talk now.'

Fortunately, when I did fade up her microphone I got it right.

DAVID WILSON *MD Southern Television*
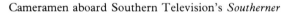
For the return of Francis Chichester, Southern Television's motor-cruiser, *Southerner*, which had an OB unit on board, really came into its own. Associated-Rediffusion hired a boat, with their people aboard, but everything went wrong with it and there was a lot of sea-sickness. The BBC had also hired a boat and shoved everything possible aboard, but they were completely at sixes and sevens, too.

Cameramen aboard Southern Television's *Southerner*

Our people, who'd had experience and training on *Southerner*, were absolutely marvellous. In spite of bad weather, we got the first pictures of Chichester back from thirty miles out to sea and delivered a three-hour networked programme that went on through the evening till the old man came ashore. When it got dark we had all the right lights aboard, so we were able to make sure the BBC didn't do so well by getting to one side and shining our lights right into the BBC cameras.

MIKE METCALFE *Engineer, Associated-Rediffusion*
On those state occasions, there'd be tremendous competition between the BBC and ITV crews for OB camera positions. I can remember one particular bit of jockeying at Princess Margaret's wedding where the Engineer in Charge was Basil Bultitude. He was one of your better Mr Fixits, but this time the Rediffusion camera was at a disadvantage compared with the BBC, because we only had a small slit in the awning for our camera to look through. This was noticed only the day before, when everything was being carefully disguised by workmen with gauze so that neither camera was obtrusive. However, legend has it that a certain amount of pound notes then passed hands. And, mysteriously, an extended slit appeared in that awning, a slit through which our lens poked to give Rediffusion some lovely shots of the Princess arriving.

ROGER APPLETON *Engineer*
Princess Margaret's wedding at Westminster Abbey was the first time Rediffusion OB cameras had used a zoom lens. It was designed to replace the turret-lenses that had to be swivelled round and although it clipped on the front in the same way as the turret, it weighed about 85 lb and was something like 2ft 6ins in length.

Our people devised a stay bar for it, but even so it seemed a bit dicey and I remember how the zoom we had on the camera up in the Abbey's organ loft looked particularly shaky. As Edward Heath happened to be sitting right underneath it, we had to rig a sort of safety-

net below the camera, so that if the lens did come
adrift there wouldn't be a major disaster during the
ceremony.

ALAN MOUNCER *Stage Manager*

The thing I'll never forget about doing Churchill's
funeral was the rehearsal. They had all the bands out
playing at four o'clock in the morning. And to show the
formation of the troops they only had the front row of
men, then – to give us the spacing – a white rope of the
appropriate length to the back row. All the carriages
were with the window-blinds down and the lamps lit. It
was like turning the clock back 200 years. They came up
Ludgate Hill to St Paul's, these marching men, and then
you'd see this rope coming up and hear the band . . .

Ceremonial occasions, however, made up only a minor
proportion of the OB Department's output. Most of its programmes were on smaller and cosier themes, as often as not
a kind of television equivalent of the family outing. Their
expeditions to zoos, circuses, parks, beauty spots and stately
homes provided viewers of that period with a more than
adequate solution to the dilemma posed by Dr Johnson's
description of the Giant's Causeway: 'worth seeing, but not
worth going to see'.

For the OB workers, themselves, there were other satisfac-
tions available.

TINY DURHAM *Sound Engineer*

We were at Woburn Abbey doing an OB about the Duke
and Duchess of Bedford and the presenter was Mary
Malcolm who was dressed, for programme reasons, in
period costume – a crinoline, lots of petticoats and those
long pantaloons – and we'd fitted her with a radio-mike
inside her clothes.

In those days, radio-mikes were a lot different from
what they are now because they needed batteries and an
aerial that went down your leg. (Today they've just
got a little bit of wire sticking out.) Well, on the last

Billy Smart on the camera with his circus

rehearsal, Mary was going round Woburn talking on about this and that when suddenly she said, 'Hold on a minute, boys', bent down, threw her skirts up and said, 'I've got to have my batteries recharged.'

DEREK BURRELL-DAVIS *Producer*
We were doing Bertram Mills' circus from Town Moor at Newcastle and the clowns were The Cairolis. As part of their performance they did a sensational *Aida*-type fanfare on great straight trumpets, so I had some special banners done for the trumpets that said 'BBC proudly presents'. But just before the show, I noticed that Francesco, the white-faced clown, still had his banner curled round his trumpet instead of letting it hang down. As it was very near starting-time I was a bit irritable, so I said to the Stage Manager, 'For heaven's sake, Francesco's an intelligent man, tell him to get his damned thing unfurled.' So the SM went over to Francesco and told him, and Francesco looked round at the camera and did a sort of 'Who, me?', but he still kept it furled. So I said to the SM, 'Tell him to get that bloody banner unfurled', and he eventually pulled it down just as I was about to start – and it read 'ITV proudly presents'.

Well, fair enough, a good gag, very funny and so on, so after the programme I had a word with another fellow in the show, a mad-professor type of clown called Don Saunders. And I sorted things out so that when Bertram Mills' circus pulled out of Newcastle and headed for their next venue at Doncaster, on the back of the last truck was a huge sign that said 'Billy Smart's Circus'.

BILL PODMORE *Cameraman*
While I was still working for ATV we did a Night Watch service for the New Year at a church in Lichfield. I was on a camera at the porch and underneath me was a bell-ringer tolling the bell. The Stage Manager was also supposed to have been in the porch to cue the bell-ringer when to stop ringing, because the moment the bell stopped the choir would come in from the vestry.

But the SM had gone over to say something to the choir and had thus got himself trapped inside the church, because now the programme had started there was no way he could come out without being seen in shot.

So the bell continued going 'Boingg, boingg, boingg' and I could hear the director on the talkback getting more and more irate. Then I noticed that the bell-rope was only just behind me. So I grabbed hold of it – which left the fellow pulling it somewhat amazed – but it did have the effect of stopping the tolling, and that gave the choir their cue and in they came. So seeing everything was now all right again I let go the rope. And there was a terrific 'Boingg'!

JIM POPLE *Film Editor*

They were doing a live OB at the zoo. As one of the cameras was being tracked along, the cameraman gave his tracker the hand-signal to stop. But nothing happened, the camera still kept going forward. So he gave a more urgent signal.

Still there's no halt, so he takes his eyes out of the view-finder and turns round to give his tracker a mouthful, only to find he's being pushed steadily forward by a giant turtle.

PETER DIMMOCK *Producer*

A live Outside Broadcast of the Royal Needlework Exhibition at St James's Palace that I produced was to include a visit from the King and Queen – the Queen Mother, as she is now. The time came for them to arrive, but they weren't there. Which was most unusual – it was very seldom the royals were late anywhere.

Fortunately we had a 'filler' planned just in case – Richard was to show us one of the rugs donated by the old Queen Mary. As was to be expected, he'd mugged up on everything about it, so I told him, 'The Queen's a little late. Better go to the rug.' He did his stuff of course and five minutes went by, then ten minutes, a quarter of an hour ... He'd practically gone into detail about every individual stitch in that darned rug, so eventually we had to leave it and get on to another prepared filler item.

I couldn't think what had happened – they only had to come down the road from Buckingham Palace – but eventually they did arrive and when the show was over, Barrie Edgar, the Stage Manager, and I were presented to the Queen. She said, 'I'm sorry I was late, Mr Dimmock. But the King and I so much enjoyed that sequence you did with Mother's rug, we were absorbed by it.'

There they had been at Buckingham Palace watching the filler we had only put on because we were desperately waiting for them to turn up. And, of course, the longer we'd stayed on that rug, the longer they would have been arriving.

DEREK BURRELL-DAVIS *Producer*
We did a whole week of OBs from Chatsworth House up in Derbyshire, all sorts of programmes, ranging from *Palace of the Peak, Music from Chatsworth* and *The Devonshire Collection* to a Chatsworth contribution to the *Out of Doors* series and an epilogue from Chatsworth Chapel. And after I'd finished what some might have described as a series of dignified commercials for the Duke of Devonshire's ancestral home, I thought there could well be an invitation from him to come in and have a drink. But there wasn't, so I set off back home and as I was driving past the gatehouse a man came out and waved me down. 'Hallo,' I thought, 'this is it. It's a message from his nibs to say thanks a million, old boy, come on over to the Dower House.'

So I pulled up and the chap said, 'Mr Burrell-Davis?'
'Yes,' I said.
'You owe us 'alf a crown for a telephone call you 'ad.'

JOAN KEMP-WELCH *Producer*
I did a Light Entertainment series for Associated-Rediffusion called *Summer Song* which came from various venues – in Scotland, down in Anglesey, out at Biggin Hill – and they were all done as OBs, no matter what the weather, with links back to the studio. I rehearsed the actors in town, then sent them out with a Floor Manager; Dougie Squires and Lenny May choreographed the

dancing; and whichever commercial company was in that region provided the cameras. One of them, I remember, had a number from a steamer coming down the Thames with everybody on deck dancing. And when, come transmission-time, it started to pour with rain, everybody just put on comic mackintoshes and hats and continued to dance.

But, for me, the most exciting one was a number we did with a singer called Kevin Scott. In the studio we showed someone's feet passing a signpost to Biggin Hill, the well known wartime airfield, then we cut to Biggin Hill itself to see Kevin Scott, dressed as an airman, walking along the now deserted runway singing about his wartime girlfriend.

ATV camera at Biggin Hill

During the song, we cut back to a mock-up of a wartime canteen in the studio, to library film of an air-raid, but we kept returning to Kevin Scott walking along the Biggin Hill runway. But this was the best bit. We had jet-planes from the RAF which took off quite a long time before the programme went on the air, with a briefing about what we wanted and when. And believe it or not – remember, this was all done live – just as Kevin Scott got to the finish of his song, those jet-planes came roaring down across the runway, then away off into the distance. What about that for timing?

4   News and Current Affairs

Back in the old days, the first newsreel
cameraman to film abroad was Charles de Jaeger. Being
multi-lingual, he spent a lot of time trying to get an
audience with the Pope. But never with any success;
the Pope was always unavailable. Finally, he was told,
'His Holiness will see you on Tuesday afternoon.' And
Charles said, 'Yes, but is he a man of his word?'
RICHARD CAWSTON *Newsreel Producer*

Some of the best overseas film shot by Charles de Jaeger in
those early days was seen in a series of programmes called
Foreign Correspondent. The main news bulletins at that time
were delivered in sound only: for the first eighteen months
after television re-opened in 1946 a radio announcer read the
news behind a picture of the BBC clock. The intention had
been to augment this with excerpts from Gaumont British,
Movietone and Pathe newsreels, but when the film industry
refused to co-operate the BBC decided to produce its own
newsreel.

The first one went out in January 1948, and it later gained
a signature tune that still occasionally surfaces in the minds
of the prematurely-grizzled – a brisk march whose title, I discovered recently, was 'Girls in Grey'. *Television Newsreel* was
seen only once a week at first, then it was stepped up to three
times, and by 1953 it was going out five times a week with a
special weekend edition. As with all other television ventures
of that era, although elements of disaster were always present
the million-to-one stroke of good luck also made an occasional
appearance.

RICHARD CAWSTON Newsreel *Producer*
For the *Weekend News Review* we used to put together
the best excerpts from the five daily newsreels, with
Richard Dimbleby linking them. In those days the labs

would only work a five-day week, so we would film Richard's links on a Friday. If there was a big national sporting event on a Saturday, there was a special dispensation by the labs and they would process it – but they wouldn't give us a dispensation to process the film of Richard's links.

So the link into, say, the Boat Race, had to be filmed before we knew the result. We would film Richard saying, 'And so Cambridge won the Boat Race for the fifty-seventh time,' or whatever; and we'd then have him say, 'And so Oxford won the Boat Race for the thirty-fourth time.'

When we did it in 1951, Richard said to me, 'What happens if there's a tie?'

I said, 'Don't be silly, there won't be a tie, it's never happened ... But, all right, let's do one extra link.'

So we did one where Richard said, 'Well, that's something nobody expected to happen' ... Next day the Oxford boat sank.

PAUL FOX Newsreel *Scriptwriter*

People sneer at the early days of *TV Newsreel* – how awful it was. It's rubbish that. Some of it no doubt was awful, but there were films – newsreel pictures from the war in Korea – which are so clearly etched in my mind that I can see them now. Pictures that Cyril Page took of bullocks being transported across the frozen river when Seoul was burning and the North Koreans were advancing. Here were the North Koreans and the Chinese coming down across the river and there were the South Korean peasants taking their bullocks over the river and putting cloth very carefully on the ice so that the bullocks could move on ...

And the time when the first contingent of British troops arrived, and the way they were greeted by the South Koreans. There was some fresh fruit there that summer, apples, and the sign on it said – I can see it clearly – 'Take few please.'

Never mind Vietnam. Korea was the first television war.

RONNIE NOBLE *Film cameraman*
There was a period in the Korean war when the most dramatic things were happening and the pictures were tremendously visual. All it needed was a fair bit of bravery and guts to get the pictures. Cyril Page did all that – no question. I did a more journalistic job. I shot features, wrote them and Paul [Fox] scripted them when he got them back to go on the air.

It was a very strange position to be that far away, writing and filming on 35 mm camera with no sound, and lugging this stuff up mountains and round hills. You packed up the film and sent it back and you never knew what happened to it. Except some time later I'd receive a letter from Paul saying, 'Such and such a story was great.'

PAUL FOX *Editor*
The first time we ever filmed in the Soviet Union was when we went over for some athletic meeting. We didn't have permission to film and all the Russians kept saying was, 'You have come here for peace and friendship.'

We said, 'We've come for the athletics meeting; could we have our passes for it?'

'No, no, you've come here for peace and friendship.'

Finally, our sound recordist, Fred Clark, he got so fed-up with waiting outside the stadium, he said, 'Peace and friendship be buggered, let's have the passes.'

What happened in the end was that we got in and filmed without actually having any filming permission. But those were the days when it was possible to film with a two-man crew.

CHARLES DE JAEGER *Film Cameraman*
I had to get some dungarees for a job. They cost £6 and I put in a bill. Administration wrote back and said, 'We are very sorry but that's not part of your job. You have to pay the bill yourself or use old clothes.' So, four or five weeks later I put in a bill: 'To entertaining Press Officer, Mr Dungarees.'

They paid without a murmur.

RONNIE NOBLE *Film Cameraman*
After I'd been in the East about a year I got a letter saying, 'Unless your expenses are justified in writing by such and such a time, you will be in trouble.' I wrote back and said, 'Great, call me home.'

Then I thought about it and I thought, 'What they want is paper.' So when I next went to the Press Club in Tokyo I said to a marvellous gang of American youngsters there from Korea, 'If you've got any bits of paper with Japanese writing on, I don't care whether it's a receipt from a brothel, a laundry, or what it is – give it to me.' And I made up a package of bits of paper with Japanese writing and I sent it with a note saying, 'Enclosed is an account of my expenses for last year.' I never heard another word.

H. W. 'JACKO' JACKSON *Sound Recordist*
In 1949, I worked on the royal tour of Australia of King George VI and Queen Elizabeth. Sir Piers Leigh was the equerry and we were invited to Buckingham Palace so that they would know us. The King said to Sir Piers, 'Does the BBC man know about paper collars?'

Sir Piers said to me, 'At formal receptions in Canberra and Sydney you will be allowed to wear stiff paper collars with your evening wear.'

Then the King said, 'Does Mr Jackson know where to get the collars from?' I didn't know, so he said, 'You go to Threshers, 140 The Strand, and tell them I sent you.'

Television Newsreel lasted till the middle of 1954, when it was succeeded by *News and Newsreel*, an uneasy amalgam whose reliance on still photographs to decorate voice-over bulletins earned it the title of 'frozen radio'. In 1955, ITN made its début, a challenge which brought about the first appearance of on-screen newsreaders. To the fascinated public, their apparent ability to look at their scripts and the viewers at the same time seemed to demonstrate an entirely new kind of reading skill.

As far as film-crews were concerned, ITN used 16 mm cameras in place of the bulkier 35 mm the BBC were hauling around, but in other respects their problems were similar.

NICK BARKER *Reporter*

A film cameraman was sent down with just a silent camera to cover a chess congress at Hastings and he was wondering how to make it visual. So he took with him a little pocket chess set, gave it to a couple of schoolboys sitting in a bus shelter and took shots of them playing. Then he gave it to a couple of old fishermen on a boat and shot them playing chess, and so on.

Later on, someone back in the news studio said, 'You were terribly lucky coming upon these fellows playing chess – it really made the story.'

The cameraman was silly enough to say, 'Oh, I fixed it.'

It was the most harmless thing to have done but he'd committed the cardinal sin: you don't fix news.

PAUL FOX *Editor*

The very first Olympic Games to be televised were the 1956 Games in Melbourne. That was at the time of Suez, the invasion of Hungary and here was the BBC in the middle of all this, the biggest national crisis since the war, about to televise the Games from Melbourne.

But one thing had been forgotten about. We hadn't got permission to film the Games. Which was why, after I left London to go to Melbourne assuming the BBC would have got permission by the time I got there, I arrived to find the BBC had decided to boycott the Games. Why did we decide to boycott them? We boycotted them because the Australians wanted us to pay. The BBC said, 'We don't pay for news.'

CHARLES DE JAEGER *Film Cameraman*

The shortest interview I ever had was with Sir Winston Churchill. He was flying to Paris for talks and at the airport I said to him, 'Will you please say a few words about what you are going to do?'

He said, 'I know what I'm going to do, young man.'
And he went in front of the camera and said, 'I am going
to Paris for talks.'

NICK BARKER
When I was sent by ITN to interview Prince Rainier,
Geoffrey Cox, who was then editor, said, 'Don't forget
to take an establishing shot of Monte Carlo showing
where you are. Just outside it, there's a sign that says,
'To Monte Carlo'. If you can stand under that, we'll
have an identifying shot.'

I got in the car with the crew, drove along the road,
turned the corner and, sure enough, there was the sign.
Standing under it was Robin Day doing a scene-setting
introduction for the BBC.

H. W. 'JACKO' JACKSON *Sound Recordist*
When Harold Wilson was made leader of the Labour
Party, in '63 I suppose it was, they sent me to Hampstead
Garden Suburb, and we set up in the front garden to
film him leaving his house. He called me in and said, 'Is
it worthwhile, all this fuss?' and I said, 'Well, sir, it is
because this is your first morning as leader.' I'd seen a
bowl of carnations in the hall, so I said, 'Before you go
out, would Mrs Wilson just pin a button-hole in your
lapel, kiss you goodbye and walk down the path?'

She did this, and we got just what we wanted. Then
ITN and all the stills men were in there – saying, 'Please!
Please do that again!' And poor Mrs Wilson had to come
out ten to twelve times to pin the same carnation into his
button-hole, and to kiss him goodbye. She said to me,
'Do you know, I've never kissed Harold so much at any
one time.'

CHARLES DE JAEGER *Film Cameraman*
I had gone on a trip to Yugoslavia with Francis Noel
Baker to get an interview with Tito, but he wouldn't give
me one. So I picked up the phone and rang Grace
Wyndham Goldie in London and said, 'I'm awfully
sorry but Marshal Tito is unable to give us an interview.
You will have to say he is unavailable, and that's all we

can do about it.'

She said, 'That's OK, Charles.'

An hour later a telephone call came through: Would we please proceed that same evening on the train to Belgrade to interview Marshal Tito next morning? Francis Noel Baker said 'How did you do it?'

I said, 'Very simple. I knew the telephones were tapped.'

Grace Wyndham Goldie is among the mythic figures of that time, a small formidable woman with one of the most original minds in the BBC hierarchy. Based in the Talks Department,

Donald Baverstock, editor of *Tonight*, with Grace Wyndham Goldie

she influenced practically every area of non-fiction television, vigorously propelling them towards innovation and expansion. So many of those she chose as her protégés are now adorning network boardrooms, I still regret my own inability to do more than shuffle my feet in her presence.

Current Affairs was one of her most energetic concerns, and never more so than in her determination to make television the prime messenger of General Election results.

ROSEMARY GILL *Production Secretary*
In 1951, I was asked to go and work for her and I can remember thinking, 'I will never be able to grapple with this,' and going into a peculiar office she had at Alexandra Palace, up some sort of little rickety stairs, all brown lino and sky-lights. She very often wore hats. I suppose it wasn't so peculiar in those days, but to me it meant a sort of status and I thought, 'Oh crumbs, a lady with a hat and clever with it.'

I did a couple of little odd jobs for her when her secretary was away and shortly after that the call came: they wanted two extra secretaries to help cover the General Election.

I had been aware in the previous weeks that the election was in the offing and that Grace Wyndham Goldie had decided that television was going for an all-out instant coverage, as was done on the radio, but hers was going to have pictures.

Her nerve takes my breath away to this day. As far as I know, entirely on her own, she had sorted out the whole television side and what it was going to look like. There wouldn't be a lot of co-operation coming from Broadcasting House; it would be done by Grace Wyndham Goldie and her secretary, a floor manager, Raymond Price, and me and another secretary, Pat Shepherd. We must have been the first special unit in television, and we moved to somewhere in Marylebone.

The job Pat and I had to do, when nomination day came, was to sort out the quickest way of getting the results onto the screen. We had no staff of a thousand then, no wall-to-wall carpet, no computers, no T-shirts ... Just me and Pat.

We found a long thing, like a pig trough, and on nomination day we got the register and we prepared caption cards for all 633 constituencies, with every permutation and combination of how the results could come out. Some constituencies, if you were lucky, had only two candidates, so it was 'Bloggs, Conservative majority, space for a number', 'Smith, Labour majority'; and then the other way round according to who had won or lost. It got complicated when you had half a dozen candidates.

We got more and more cards in our pig trough and one caption artist wrote the whole lot – 6,000 or something. I don't know how he did it – from when the names are officially announced I think it's only a fortnight or three weeks.

Grace had both studios A and B, and Richard Dimbleby was in A, entirely on his own, to convey all the results, with David Butler with a slide-rule – no computers – working out statistics and the swings and predictions. I think there was some kind of a swingometer and David brought with him ten students as runners.

Richard Dimbleby and David Butler

At the other end of Studio A was the caption artist with a step-ladder and a pot of black paint. He didn't even have Magimarkers in those days; the paint was wet.

There was one artist up a ladder filling in the map, and one putting the figures on our cards.

In Studio B was our actual pig trough and the students. The only way Grace was able to arrange to get the results, because the Broadcasting House facilities were very over-burdened and not quite prepared to pass anything on, was by a couple of daffodil telephones, antiquated even in those days, linked to either Reuters or the Press Association.

The students jotted down the results from Reuters on a piece of paper, Pat and I scrabbled through our pig trough, found the appropriate card, pencilled on the figures, gave them to a caption artist who slopped the wet paint on, and we took it in turns to rush them to the next-door studio and put them on an easel. And, do you know, we got our results out faster than radio because, for obvious reasons, nothing was double-checked – because we had no means of doing so. But we only made one mistake.

We stayed on the air much as now until the early hours of the morning and came back again first thing until about half-past eleven. That early technical equipment got so hot – mainly because of all the lights – it should have blown up. We did fry an egg on one piece of equipment just to see if it would, and it did.

What places that 1951 election broadcast so high on the list of forgotten excitements is that it gave many viewers their first demonstration that television could communicate as quickly and efficiently as radio. It seems to have brought in only one letter of complaint, which Grace Wyndham Goldie passed on to Rosemary Gill.

ROSEMARY GILL
It came because, the programme being on the air non-stop, the only time we fed Richard and David was when we were able to crawl into the set and lob sandwiches and coffee over the desks while the captions were being shown. So, as far as the viewers were concerned, Richard was never seen to get any food.

This lady wrote in complaining, 'How appalling that the poor man should be broadcasting continuously, and late into the night, and not so much as a drink of water!'

'The art of the possible adjusting to the art of the passable' was how somebody described that period when politics and television were still getting used to each other. Indeed, in the days when Roland Fox was employed to patrol the Westminster beat, care was always taken to describe him as 'our Parliamentary Correspondent'; not, as he would have been billed in any of the newspapers, 'Political Correspondent'. In the eyes of the BBC at that time, the very word 'political' smacked of the shady and the partisan. Seen against that kind of cautiousness, some of the bolder strategems news and current affairs people resorted to seem even more worthy of note.

ROLAND FOX *Assistant Parliamentary Correspondent*
The early broadcasts we did from Westminster had to be done to the 'Roving Eye' camera. They sent this great mobile camera-van down into Parliament Square, got special permission from the police, and either Teddy Thompson or I would go outside onto the pavement, hotfoot from the debate, and solemnly say our piece into a camera mounted on the top of this huge van – crowds collecting the while.

The first time we used the Roving Eye was one night during some national crisis and Teddy was doing a very powerful piece. There were a few minutes to spare and Teddy went out into Parliament Square and walked up and down the pavement looking at his script. Then, from Alexandra Palace, they called him to stand-by. To my horror he screwed up his notes, threw them in the gutter and just said his piece to the camera.

At that stage of television, in the dark, there on the pavement surrounded by a crowd of people, it was a feat of great courage.

The Roving Eye

ANDREW GARDNER *Newscaster*

We were awaiting the resignation of George Brown who was then in the Labour Party cabinet. His rows reached a point where it looked as if his resignation was imminent.

We had waited and waited, and Julian Haviland was down at the Commons and was going to telephone this information direct to our control room, because we expected it to happen while *News at Ten* was still on-air.

We got nearer and nearer to the end of the programme, but still no news about George Brown and we were desperate to be the first to announce this. When we were about twenty seconds from the end of the programme, I heard a phone ring in the control room – we wear earpieces, so we can hear what's going on in there – and I heard my producer say, 'Ah, he's gone, Julian! Right!' So without my desk telephone ringing I picked it up and said, 'Well, let's see if there is any late news' – nobody ever mentioned to me afterwards that it was odd that I picked it up when it hadn't rung – and I said down the telephone, 'Really? Good heavens!' Then I put it down and said to the camera, 'I've just heard that George Brown has resigned.'

ROLAND FOX *Assistant Parliamentary Correspondent*

In the mid-fifties, the time came when it was thought there ought to be some kind of studio at Westminster. So whenever Teddy Thompson and I had a few minutes to spare we used them to see if we could find somewhere suitable.

Eventually we found a tiny basement room in a block opposite Big Ben in Bridge Street, two storeys down from ground level. That became the first remotely controlled television studio in the BBC.

When they wanted to do a piece from us for television all we had to do was to go down into this basement studio, unlock the door, switch on a light and that switched everything on. The studio became live, the camera was live and from Alexandra Palace they were able to control the camera. It had a limited amount of movement. We sat down at the desk and saw a camera focusing, and there was a telephone link, so we were able to do live inserts into the news bulletins.

On one occasion, I went over to do a piece, I can't remember for what. They gave me the go-ahead, but I no sooner started when all the lights went out. I kept talking, because those pieces were only about two minutes long, and by the time you'd typed and read them through a few times you knew them roughly. So I continued talking. The lights came on again, went out again, but I just ploughed on. When I finished my piece the telephone rang immediately and the producer said, 'Thank God you kept talking, Roland, because we lost vision but the sound was still going out!'

PAUL FOX *Head of Current Affairs*

Kennedy assassination night ... It was a Friday and everybody else had gone to the BAFTA Awards at the Dorchester. I was still at Lime Grove so I was the one who got the news. My concern was to do a special 'tribute' programme, and I was quite clear what I wanted for this: I wanted the Prime Minister, who was Sir Alec Douglas-Home; I wanted Harold Wilson, who was the leader of the opposition; and I wanted Jo Grimond, the Liberal leader.

And then it became a question of *getting* those three. Alec Home was on his way to spend the weekend with the Duke of Norfolk, and certainly to my knowledge had not heard that Kennedy was dead. He was stopped by the police on the way to Arundel and told about it, and the tribute. He turned around and, because he was in his country clothes, went back to Number Ten, changed, and went to Broadcasting House. He was going to appear before the cameras in the small television studio they've got there, but when he arrived he got stuck in the lift for half an hour.

Harold Wilson was addressing a meeting in North Wales, but we managed somehow to find him and he drove to our studio at Manchester. Jo Grimond was at the Oxford Union, so we sent one of our fastest drivers to bring him back to Lime Grove studios.

Richard Dimbleby was not very well, so I phoned Ian Trethowan and he came in to link the programme. So now we had Ian in Studio H at Lime Grove with Lord Chalfont, who was then Alun Gwynne Jones, the Defence Correspondent of *The Times*; and we had the PM, Sir Alec Douglas-Home, stuck in a lift at Broadcasting House, Harold Wilson in Manchester and Jo Grimond being driven back from Oxford. It turned out one hell of a programme.

Whatever difficulties people may have experienced putting together news and current affairs programmes in London, they had an easy ride compared to their colleagues in what the BBC would indulgently refer to as 'the Regions'. When Manchester began making its own local programmes in 1957, all they had for studios were two converted chapels. (Fortunately, one of them still had an inscription over the door that read 'Where there is no vision, the people shall perish.')

JIM ENTWHISTLE *Assistant News Editor, Manchester*
The men who put Manchester's rather rudimentary
early news pictures on the air had to descend rickety
stairs to 'the crypt'. The taller ones had to stoop, but
sometimes forgot. . . .

Our short pieces of film were rushed to us by car from
an attic over a shop in Deansgate, where three enterpris-
ing photographers had launched a film and processing
business to meet the BBC demand.

ALAN PROTHEROE *News Editor, BBC Wales*
When we started Welsh television in Cardiff – in both
languages – the number of staff was tiny, the equipment
was primitive beyond measure and every single bit of it
came out from the redundant plant stores. The studio
was so small that the camera could only move right or
left; no way could it go forward. In fact, it couldn't really
move much in any direction because the dolly only had
three out of the four wheels.

We would shoot black-and-white film in Cardiff and
it would be processed by a freelance in what looked like
a cocktail-shaker. He would then spread it over a clothes-
horse and dry it with a hair-dryer. After editing the film,
he would have to send it to Bristol, because Cardiff had
no film transmission equipment.

We'd record the commentary on disc in Cardiff and
– 'live', on-air – we'd ring up Bristol on a field telephone
(you actually had to crank the handle) and tell them to
run the film.

On the picture feed from Bristol to Cardiff we'd watch
the numbers coming down, and as they got to zero, the
Studio Manager would start the disc with the commentary and effects. Sometimes, because of mains fluctua-
tions between the two cities, the disc had to be speeded
up a bit.

Looking back now, people say, 'Well, of course it
couldn't have happened.' But I was there, and it happened like that twice a day, regularly.

JAMES CELLAN JONES *Producer*
I was once in the Cardiff studios when they were doing
a lunch-time programme in Welsh and the Floor
Manager was tearing about the place saying, 'We're in
terrible trouble, boy. The programme's about the
Cyprus situation and nobody knows the Welsh for
"compromise".'

YVONNE LLOYD *Production Assistant*
One of the things we showed on *Day by Day* in the first
week of Southern TV was a smallholding in Storrington
at which Jomo Kenyatta had worked as a weeder.

And we used to have a lot of action inside that studio
in those days. At pantomime time we had Julian Pettifer
flying across the studio on wires, and on other occasions
we managed to get an elephant, a chimpanzee, a double-
decker bus and a football team in there. It was all very
unpredictable. You would be up in the control gallery
and find something or somebody in the studio nobody
had told you about: students climbing over the cameras
and so on. But you had to cope with it and it was great
fun, because it was live and it was all new.

ALAN PROTHEROE *News Editor, BBC Wales*
We had a distinguished man declare war. He was a very
fine character, Mervyn Jones, chairman of the Wales
Gas Board – known, of course, as 'Jones the Gas'.

It was during a very bad winter, when the gas supplies
were at a critically low level, and we had transmitted
several appeals from the Gas Board to conserve gas. I
decided to put Mervyn on live to top the regional programme, introducing him as chairman of the Wales Gas
Board. Mervyn leaned forward into the camera and said,
'War has been declared.'

He did a dramatic pause, then went on to explain,
'What I mean is, war has been declared on the weather.'

Now Mervyn really was a very distinguished man. If
he told you Sunday was Monday you would believe him.
And many elderly folk did. So much so, they simply
stopped listening after hearing him say, 'War has been

declared.' Our switchboard was so jammed, it seized up.

We had to do an additional piece at the end of the programme, where Mervyn explained, 'I was only talking about war on the *weather*.'

Of course, the chairman of the Wales Gas Board was by no means the only major political figure to crop up in the recollections of those who worked in news and current affairs. If that branch of live television gave its employees any advantage over the rest of us, it was the opportunity to be unimpressed by the impressive.

JAMES CELLAN-JONES *Assistant Floor Manager*

There was a Floor Manager, John Day, who always retained his Cockney characteristics no matter who came to the studio. When Mr Harold Macmillan came, there were a lot of people in blue suits saying, 'Yes, Chancellor, no, Chancellor'. But Johnny said to him, 'Right, cock, over 'ere. Boys, give me a piece of Duke of York,' and on the marvellous blue carpet he scrawled a band of white chalk.

'Right, that's where you put your daisy roots. Now, you look at that camera, and you go "blah-blah-blah-blah". Then they've got a caption, you look at it, then you go "blah-blah-blah-blah" again. Right?'

A mesmerised Macmillan simply nodded, and did it. Later, Anthony Eden sent in a request, 'Can John Day be present when I do my broadcast?'

ALASTAIR BURNET *Newscaster*

Two things are never in short supply when the great come to the studios to be interviewed: senior executives and fashionable drinks. (Prince Philip has been known to examine the array of bottles and then ask cheerfully for a beer.) Harold Macmillan, in turn, made his entrances playing one or other of his many parts. An early favourite when he was Prime Minister was to pretend that he was just a sleepy-eyed old bookseller, baffled by the hyper-sophisticated world of television. He looked

Floor Manager Joan Marsden ('Mum') cues Sir Anthony Eden

apprehensive, and his voice dropped. So much so that when asked what he would like to drink, he was virtually inaudible amid the chatter of the senior executives all around.

The butler tried again, 'Champagne, Glenmorangie, Remy Martin?' (He actually liked Dimple Haig.)

Another inaudible reply.

'Bourbon, perhaps, or Highland Park, or Glenlivet or even Vodka?'

Summoning all his strength, the old bookseller made himself heard: 'I keep asking for the way to the loo.'

STEPHEN HEARST *Director*

I was asked by Grace Wyndham Goldie to prepare an obituary of Sir Anthony Eden, who at that time was gravely ill. One of the politicians we interviewed was Lord Attlee. We went to collect him by car from the Athenaeum and Grace Wyndham Goldie came with me in order to brief him, but she couldn't go into the Athenaeum because she was a woman. I went in to collect him, and on the way to the small Kensington studios Grace

explained that she wanted a recollection of Eden from
their War Cabinet days together, and then a recollection
from when Labour was in opposition. There was no
reaction at all from Attlee. He just puff-puffed on his
pipe.

When we got to the studios I told him I would like
three minutes in all. I would do a long shot – he nodded
and went on puffing – then a mid-shot, and he nodded
and went on puffing.

He did it all perfectly. It was all over within about
eight minutes and as we still had the car, I said to him,
'Where would you like to go, sir?'

He said, 'Going to India tomorrow. Need a bag. The
Army and Navy Stores.'

ROLAND FOX *Parliamentary Correspondent*
I was the first broadcasting chairman of the Parliamentary Press Gallery and for our annual dinners we
always tried to get the Prime Minister of the day, which
I did. It was Harold Macmillan and after the dinner we
went into the Press Gallery precincts for our entertainment. We'd got together quite a nice panel of artists, and
I'd persuaded Stanley Unwin to be MC. He also did a
turn, a bit of political gibberish, of course, and it had
Dorothy Macmillan hooting with laughter.

After a while there was a pause, and during the hush
Harold Macmillan said, 'I can't understand a word the
fellow's saying.'

ALASTAIR BURNET *Newscaster*
Of course, Macmillan was up to all the tricks – and more.
So was Harold Wilson. He had been having a bad run
with the pound in his pocket or something, so there were
some mildly difficult things to be answered, including
calls for him to resign.

'Fifteen seconds to transmission,' said the Floor
Manager, then, 'Ten seconds.'

Wilson leaned over and said, 'You know, Alastair,
Mary was very pleased by that charming and generous
notice you gave to her new poems. She's most grateful,
and so am I.'

'On-air,' said the Floor Manager.
But not quite the moment to call for so kindly a man's
resignation.

STEPHEN HEARST *Producer*
At the time of the visit of Khrushchev and Bulganin,
Khrushchev's son-in-law, Adjubei, who was then
Editor of *Izvestia*, came to the Television Centre with
a party. They were given dinner by Grace Wyndham
Goldie and, in customary Russian fashion, Adjubei
arrived at the hospitality suite inside the Television
Centre with a huge bunch of flowers, which he gallantly
handed to her.

Much later Grace found out he had actually taken
them from a stand near the reception area. Presumably
he had forgotten flowers and just went for the nearest –
the BBC's own flowers.

GEORGE CAMPEY *Television Publicity Officer*
Senator Nixon and his wife came to an occasion at Lime
Grove, I think just after Hugh Greene had become
Director General. There was a BBC photographer and
one rota photographer from Fleet Street there to take
some pictures of Nixon who at that precise moment was
then holding a glass of wine.

Mrs Nixon saw this and took it out of his hand. She
said to me, 'You can always offend somebody if you are
seen with a glass in your hand. If you are not seen with
one you can offend nobody.'

BILL PARKINSON *Floor Manager*
Albert Stevenson, a long-time Light Entertainment pro-
ducer, and for many years responsible for the Light
Entertainment Auditions Unit, started as a Floor
Manager, and at one time was on *Panorama*.

One afternoon rehearsal they were lining up shots and
because they wanted to get a sound-level for an item
where Francis Williams would be interviewing Dag
Hammarskjöld, the Secretary-General of the United
Nations, the producer asked Albert to 'stand-in' for
him.

Stand-ins during the rehearsal of a political discussion

For real

Francis Williams said, 'Tell me, Mr Hammarskjöld, how did you come to be appointed Secretary-General to the United Nations?'

Albert said, 'Well, I was unemployed at the time, and as I was walking down the road one day this geezer comes up to me and says, "How'd you like to be Secretary-General of the United Nations, mate?"'

Albert Stevenson takes time out from rehearsal

Now Grace Wyndham Goldie was in the gallery at the time and she came down into the studio and tore a strip off Albert, good and proper, for this. But Dag Hammarskjöld had arrived somewhat unexpectedly a few minutes before, so the sound-man said, 'OK, shall we have the interviewee himself in the chair for a sound-level check?'

So Mr Hammarskjöld was sat in the chair, and Francis Williams asked, 'How did you come to be appointed Secretary-General?'

And Dag Hammarskjöld said, in a mixture of Swedish and Cockney, 'Well, I was walking down the road one day, and this geezer comes up to me. . . .'

Panorama began in 1953 as a fortnightly magazine programme, only lightly topical, with regular reviews of books and films. When Richard Dimbleby became its presenter in 1955, it changed what one of its early FM's persisted in calling its 'floormat', justifying its claim to be 'a weekly window on the world' by concentrating on informed comment and high-level discussion.

PAUL FOX *Editor,* Panorama
One of the most memorable *Panoramas* was when Ludovic Kennedy interviewed President Kennedy. They knew each other, because at a press conference when Kennedy had been nominated Democratic presidential candidate and Ludo had to give his name, he said 'Kennedy, BBC *Panorama*'.

Jack Kennedy said, 'A very useful name to have.'

Later, when Kennedy came to London on a private visit he didn't want to do any interviews. But I asked Ludo to try to do a doorstep interview. We had the use of OB cameras outside the Radziwill's house where he was staying. There was Ludo doorstepping, and after dinner when Kennedy came out, there 'live' into *Panorama* came this interview between Ludo and the President. Memorable. Beautiful and 'live'.

JOAN MARSDEN *Floor Manager*
Whenever American VIPs came to the studios they were of course accompanied by a large number of security guys. For instance, when Vice-President Hubert Humphrey came to *Panorama* there were about twenty security men and they wanted to search everyone and everything coming into the studio, including a briefcase standing to one side.

I said, 'You can't touch that, it's Robin Day's.'

They said, 'We don't care whose it is. Anything could

be in there.'

I said, 'For heaven's sake, it's just his dirty shirts, I expect.' And, sure enough, when they opened it out they fell ...

Richard Dimbleby in *Panorama*

PAUL FOX

When Woodrow Wyatt went to British Leyland – Austin, as it was then – to cover a strike meeting for *Panorama*, he was greeted rather noisily by the strikers. The gates were barred to him, he couldn't drive in and they gave him a really bad time.

Woodrow couldn't understand it. After all, he used to be the local MP there; why was he being treated in this unpleasant way?

The cameraman said, 'You must know why they're giving you a hard time.'

Woodrow said, 'No, why?'

He was driving a Mercedes.

JOAN MARSDEN
Who was that very large gentleman who was Minister of Education? An item in *Panorama* went wrong and I had to get the next interviewee on, so I literally threw him across the studio ... Edward Boyle, that's who it was. I threw him across the studio. Afterwards I got a letter from the PRO, who was John Harris, who later became Lord Harris, thanking me for throwing a peer of the realm into *Panorama*.

PAUL FOX *Head of Current Affairs*
The night of the Cuba crisis was a momentous one. There was a view that hostilities would start the next day, and we did a special *Panorama* that night. And after we had announced, 'There will be a special *Panorama*, with Richard Dimbleby dealing with the Cuban missile crisis,' a viewer phoned up who was very persistent; so persistent that eventually somehow she got put through to me.

She said, 'I am just an ordinary woman viewer and all I want to hear from tonight's programme is one thing. This is what I want Richard Dimbleby to tell me: is it safe for my child to go to school tomorrow?'

And that was exactly the question we had Richard ask Lord Chalfont.

Another of *Panorama*'s claims on our memory must be the night they pulled off the most successful spoof in TV history. On 1 April 1957, the full Dimbleby gravitas was lent to a concluding item purporting to be a filmed report of the annual spaghetti harvest in a typical Italian spaghetti orchard.

It was agreeable to discover that the idea for it came from Charles de Jaeger, the cameraman who was the subject of the first item in this chapter. He was able to supply details of the massive technical problems attendant upon loading a tree with spaghetti.

CHARLES DE JAEGER *Film Cameraman*

Panorama's April the first famous spaghetti harvest came from my school-days in Austria, when a master was always saying to us, 'You're so stupid you'd think spaghetti grew on trees.' So it had always been in my mind to do the story and I tried for several years. It was not until I was working on *Panorama* that I got the go-ahead.

I went to the Swiss Tourist Office, who said they would help, and I flew to Lugano. It was in March when I thought the weather would be sunny with flowers out. There was a mist over the whole area.

The tourist office guy took me around all over the place; not one blossom out, no leaves out. It was now Tuesday and I could not find anything and said in desperation, 'What can be done?'

Then we found this hotel in Castiglione, which had laurel trees with leaves on, tall trees. So I said, 'We'll do it here. Let's go down into Lugano and get some hand-made spaghetti.'

Drying the spaghetti

We did that, put the strands of spaghetti in a big wooden platter, took that in the car and we drove back. By the time we got there, the damn things wouldn't hang up. They'd dried out. So we cooked them, tried to put them on the trees, and this time they fell off because they were so slippery.

Hanging the spaghetti

Then this tourist guy had a brilliant idea – put the spaghetti between damp cloths. That worked and we got local girls to hang them up – about ten pounds' worth. Then we got the girls into national costume and filmed them climbing on ladders with these baskets, filling them up, and then laying them out in the sun. And we said in the script, with a guitar playing in the background, 'We have this marvellous festival. The first harvest of the spaghetti.'

At the end of the three-minute film Richard Dimbleby said, 'Now we say goodnight on this first day of April.' In spite of that hint, next morning it was surprising the number of people who hadn't twigged.

5 Arts and Props

> In George Foa's production of *La Bohème*, he had a
> Greek Mimi and there was an Australian tenor who kept
> getting his head in shot. George, directing in the gallery,
> cried to the cameraman, 'I am so sorry, he's a bloody
> tenor' – as if that explained everything.
> STEPHEN BUNDY *Designer*

The engaging and energetic George Foa, born in Milan, was
a pioneer in bringing opera to television. After his *La Bohème*
it was not only viewers who were at pains to let him know that

George Foa

it was the first opera they had ever watched; a number of BBC staff went out of their way to tell him the same thing. He was fond of recounting how a secretary said to him the following morning, 'I thought the story was very good, but what I specially liked was the background music.'

Opera programmes were the province of television's Music and, later, Arts Department, whose other preoccupations included ballet, concerts, recitals and trying to wrestle a peak-time spot from Light Entertainment. Although, like every area of television, it lived under the constant threat of everything degenerating into complete confusion at any moment, many of the ground-rules it set down are still observed today. 'Where opera is concerned,' decreed George Foa, 'Television simply cannot continue the tradition of fat prima donnas. What's more, singers must be able to do without the help of a conductor.'

This last was partly to avoid problems with 'eye-line' – i.e., artists peering in the wrong direction – but it was mainly because the orchestra would probably be in a different studio. Nor was that the only difficulty encountered when high culture tangled with high technology.

VERA SETON-REID *Vision-mixer*
> We did a production called *Paris Soir*, a sort of *opéra bouffe* with a snow scene. They scrumpled up Florapac for snow, took it up to the lighting gantry and shook it down. Suddenly all the noses were sneezing, just as someone was going to take a high C. We weren't allowed to use that again.

STEWART MARSHALL *Designer*
> There was a donkey in a George Foa opera, a male donkey, which showed its masculinity throughout rehearsal, making large tracks in the peat which we'd laid on the floor of Studio G. He'd calmed down by transmission though.

MAGGIE SAUNDERS *Assistant Floor Manager*
> When I became an AFM we did a live *Cavalleria Rusticana*, where they sing the Nuns' Chorus. We had a children's chorus and because it wasn't a music cue they

didn't know where to come in. George Foa got me to dress up as a nun in voluminous black, with a score tucked in underneath my bosom to give the cue. On transmission the entire score fell from beneath my clothing and clattered onto the studio floor.

ELIZABETH AGOMBAR *Costume Designer*
For me the most interesting opera I ever did was *La Vide Brêve*, directed by Basil Coleman. It was the first opera in colour, and it had Margaret Price right at the beginning of her career. I remember the production with, I think, more pleasure than almost anything, not just because I had a ball doing the costumes but because I really did design them all and it was a lovely thing to do.

One problem we had which I think they don't suffer from very much now was the curious thing that used to happen with lighting in those early colour days. Certain colours came out in the most unexpected ways and you never quite knew how they would be affected. One of my most carefully worked-out colour schemes, involving principals and extras, was the wedding scene, for which I'd very carefully blended all the costumes so as to get a lovely overall picture. Which it was, except for one grey dress which came out on the screen a bright green. Stuck out like a sore thumb.

Helping to mount television's early Arts programmes would seem to have been no job for anyone born with a highly developed sense of setback. However, the work did offer various incidental felicities, chief among which was privileged contact with the great ones of that world.

JACK KINE *Scenic Artist*
Everybody came to television, Paul Robeson, Margot Fonteyn ... I particularly remember Margot Fonteyn, because I got covered in her sweat one night. I was in there painting scenery, and she came spinning off and sprayed me.

Maria Callas in *Chelsea at Nine*

MAUREEN WINSLADE *Make-up Assistant*

Suddenly the world came to television. Sir Thomas
Beecham and his orchestra came. In those days the
cameras used to 'peel', and many of the orchestra were
so bald-headed we couldn't just go round to each and
every one and powder their pates – that was too obvious.
So we just said: 'Would all the bald-headed men please
come to Make-up?'

It was their first experience of it. They queued up and
decided coming to Make-up was really quite nice.

BABETTE LORAINE *Make-up Assistant*

Musicians needed to be made up like everyone else, of
course. You had to be careful of fiddlers though, because
you couldn't have grease anywhere near where their
fiddles rested on their chins.

MAGGIE SAUNDERS *Producer's Secretary*
When Sir Thomas Beecham and the Royal Philharmonic turned up for rehearsal, he said slowly and very deliberately, 'I will go through the programme once, beginnings and ends. Then we will go over to the bar.'

So we did a kind of rehearsal, mainly topping and tailing, but we did go right through one short piece and we completely lost our way in the score. In the gallery, I said to Phillip Bate, our producer, 'They must have made a cut somewhere. We'll have to find out where it is.' He said, 'Well, you go down to the studio and sort it out.'

Even though I could read a score and knew what I was talking about, I thought, 'Oh, God! With all those musicians looking at me I've got to go down and talk about music to Tommy Beecham, and he is a bit of a tearaway.'

Anyway, I suddenly spied someone at the back of the orchestra: I think he was the leader of the second violins, a chap I'd met during the war, an Austrian Jew who'd been interned, then went in the Pioneer Corps. I don't think he remembered me, but because I remembered him I said, 'Could you tell me where the cut is?' He said, 'Yes,' and we got it sorted out.

But it was because of him I found the confidence to talk to those kind of people. We were very young then, you know, and we had no experience of those big names in music or drama or variety. But when they came to the television medium, they had to do what we told them to, because they had no idea what was going on.

ROS POOL *Production Secretary*
When we did *Picture Page* the people we interviewed on the afternoon show were different from those on the evening show. On one occasion, a man came in during the afternoon with a ring-tailed lemur, a kind of monkey, and it was supposed to be removed after the programme. But in the evening Segovia walked into his dressing-room to find a ring-tailed lemur admiring itself in the mirror.

DAVID STEVENS *Press Officer, ATV*
As a gesture to the then ITA in the mid-sixties, we put on a *Golden Hour* – opera, ballet, and general arts. It ran two and a half hours, with people like O'Toole doing a soliloquy from *Hamlet*, Fonteyn and Nureyev in *Swan Lake*, and on one particular occasion Maria Callas and Tito Gobbi with the aria from the third act of *Tosca.* At the rehearsal at Covent Garden, knowing how difficult Maria Callas was with photographers and what terrible scenes there could be, I warned Lew Grade.

He said, 'I don't care. Get the boys in.' So I got the boys in and there they all were in the front row of the stalls with their Hasselblads, and three rows back was Lew. Gobbi and Callas came on with the opening music of Act Three, for the scene where she stabs Scarpia, and she starts to sing. She couldn't see all that clearly from the stage, but she felt there was some movement down there, and suddenly she raised her arm and said, 'Stop! Either they go, or I go.'

And Lew looked astonished and shouted to me, 'Get those photographers out of here!' So I did. But they'd got all the shots they wanted for some super spreads in the next day's tabloids.

MICHAEL BOND *Cameraman*
I worked on a programme series with Tito Gobbi. Someone like Gobbi really wants to produce the whole thing because he's done so much. He'll see some little old extra carrying a lamp across the background and he'll stop everything and say, 'No, you don't carry a lamp like that. You carry it like this . . .'

PADDY RUSSELL *Floor Manager*
Gian Carlo Menotti came over for *The Saint of Bleeker Street* and we brought the American cast over, too. Menotti came to the studio to watch the live transmission. Afterwards, he came tearing down the stairs from the control gallery in tears. It was wonderful.

TINY DURHAM *Engineer*

We went into Maida Vale 1 studio for the first time with television. Yehudi Menuhin was the soloist, and that day, when we had our rehearsal break with a cup of tea, Menuhin came down and sat on the floor and played the violin to the boys all around him.

PADDY RUSSELL

I remember working on *Salome* with Helga Pilarchezk, who was, I think I'm right in saying, the leading soprano in Hamburg, and a lovely lady. In *Salome* she did her own dancing which was unusual, and Gillian Lynne, of now considerable fame, did the choreography. I loved music, but Mozart was my big love, and I had never come across Strauss before, and I found it very difficult.

Helga was watching me, and one lunch-break she came over to me and said, 'You are finding it difficult?' and I said, 'Yes, I am.'

She said, 'But it's so easy,' and she spent her lunch-break at the piano teaching me that Strauss is all themes, motifs, most of them only five or six notes. She played them to me and she said, 'That's mine, and that's Jokanan. That's Herod, and that's Herodias.'

She said, 'If you listen you will realise that what Strauss does is, he blends them. Once you have got those very simple themes, then you will know the rest of the opera.' It was a whole new world to me, and I have loved Strauss ever since.

BILL WARD *Producer*

Eric Robinson was a very nice man to work with. At the time of the death of King George VI, the TV service closed down for forty-eight hours and Cecil McGivern was in charge of programmes. The King died on the Thursday I think and McGivern said, 'Would you open up with a suitable programme? Something not too serious but on the other hand we can't have comedy. It must be entertaining, must have music, be in keeping with the occasion, but not miserable. And you have forty-eight hours to put it together.'

So we put together a two-hour-plus programme. We

Eric Robinson

had somebody dancing *Spectre de la Rose*; we had Greig's No. 1 piano concerto; we did a medley of sailor songs, because George VI was a sailor; we did Lotte Reiniger doing some music to her silhouette puppets; we set music to the Interlude, *June Night on Marlow Reach*, and we played some music to a boat going down river.

And Eric hosted it. Though he had appeared in the jazz programme, that was his very first appearance as a presenter of a programme. It was from there that *Music For You* evolved.

ELIZABETH AGOMBAR *Costume Designer*
Music For You was a programme that went out live, which presented no end of problems, particularly with those big operatic stars. They wouldn't come over until the day of transmission and if you were required to provide clothes for them you had to do it from the measurements they sent to you, cross your fingers and trust in the Lord.

Lime Grove Wardrobe Mistress, Mrs Copley, searching through Wardrobe Stores

On one wonderful occasion they sent me the measurements all in centimetres, and when I worked it out the singer was sixty inches from the waist to the ground.

That occurred while *Music For You* was being produced by Patricia (Paddy) Foy. Television's youngest woman producer, she took over the programme while she was still in her early twenties. After serving as George Foa's assistant, she won equal acclaim as a Music Department innovator, particularly for the series of celebrity recitals she produced. Moiseiwitch, for example, only consented to appear on television under two conditions, the first being that he had Paddy as his producer.

Patricia Foy

PADDY FOY *Music Producer*

The second condition was that Harry Pepper, Doris Arnold and Ronnie Waldman came along and played poker with him right up until the last moment. Very, very nice, and he was always so charming.

I had inherited this concept of cutting on each musical phrase. George Barnes, Director of Television, would never press his point of view, but gave his opinion about the noisy thoughts that were provoked by all that cutting. So one day, just for the hell of it, I had this Moiseiwitch recital and I thought I will do the whole programme on a developing shot with one camera.

Two people were absolutely delighted with it, both of whom I respected. One was George Barnes, who sent me a memo: 'You proved it could be done', and Michael

Barry also sent a memo: 'I hope you never look back.'

Those two things fortified me enormously. When he left, George Barnes said to me: 'Thank you for bringing repose to our screens.'

Paddy Foy was also renowned for her ballet programmes, at a time when viewers tended to look upon ballet somewhat guardedly. It had first been televised in the blue-lipstick days of 1936 and Felicity Gray's *Ballet For Beginners* had helped break down a lot of resistance. Nevertheless, in 1956, a programme journal could still give prominences to the following letter from a viewer in Coulsdon, Surrey:

> While not wishing to contradict your correspondent in her statement about low necklines on television, I would consider the costume of male ballet dancers of greater importance. The tights they appear to have been poured into surely come into the category of abusing the privilege which we allow them in coming into our homes.

Coincidentally, there were members of ballet's backroom staff who could also claim to have suffered abuses of privilege.

FRANK HOLLAND *Clerk*

I used to dread it when we were allocated to do a ballet because in those days the designers did the sets and also the costumes. I was the young clerk outside the designers' office and Stephen Bundy, who used to do music and ballet-type programmes, once called me in and said, 'I wonder if you would be so kind, I wonder if you would wear this leotard for me while I paint it?'

I started to put it on and he said, 'No, no. You have to take your trousers off.' So I took my trousers off, and then he said, 'Frank, would you now stand up on the chair here so I can paint it?'

The south-east wing of Alexandra Palace windows were very huge, down to the floor, overlooking the park. And there I was, to the amazement of the passing public, standing on a chair wearing tights while Stephen painted me.

We got to lunch-time, and Stephen said, 'OK, Frank. We'll continue after lunch.'

I looked outside for my trousers, not wanting to go to the canteen in a leotard, and the lads I was working with had hidden them just for a bit of fun. From then onwards I always tried to keep out of the way when we put on a ballet.

CYRIL WILKINS *Cameraman*

We used to have ballets and full-size orchestras in those little studios in Ally Pally. And to track far enough back to get a long shot we'd have to get the camera right amongst the violins. The producer would say, 'Right, track back, the little swans are coming on.' We'd go roaring back and those chaps in the orchestra would scatter like mad.

JIM POPLE *Director*

For the opening of Rediffusion's Studio 5, the largest in Europe, they did a monumental production of *Scheherezade*. Because the whole studio was designed as a vast great stage, Floor Managers and certain other production people dressed in costume so that they could mingle.

In one market scene an FM spots a beggarly-looking individual leaning against a corner and not doing very much, so he goes over to him and says, 'Act! Move around a bit. Look as if you're doing something.'

The beggar opens his filthy robes to reveal an effects-microphone and says, 'Go away, I'm one of us.'

ROSEMARY GILL *Assistant Floor Manager*

I was working on a play when I got a telephone call: 'Nip down to such-and-such a rehearsal room' – it was a church hall somewhere – 'because they've got the *Nutcracker* ballet in rehearsal there. They've already been rehearsing it for a fortnight, it goes into the studio next week, and their AFM has just gone off sick.'

Well, I went down there and it was Margot Fonteyn and Michael Soames. Marvellous – I was all agog. But as there were still a few days of rehearsal to go and I didn't know the ballet, I thought that for the first day I'd just stick around and watch.

Now, when you were an AFM on a ballet, one of the first things you did was draw the main details of the set on the rehearsal-room floor with camera tape. But then came the hardest part – plotting the dance-lines the choreographer worked out during rehearsal. And you did that by marking them on the floor with differently coloured tapes. You then had to copy those on to your plan of the studio floor, so that when you got in there you could reproduce the dance-lines for the benefit of the cameras.

It was never an easy job, and especially not on this *Nutcracker*, because its set had rows of great columns in it, with all the dance-diagonals worked out between the columns. So it wasn't something I was looking forward to, and after watching the dancing for a day I thought, I really must put my mind to checking what's gone down on the studio-plan – it could take quite some time.

But when I looked at the plan I'd got from the AFM I was replacing, I saw it had 15 columns down one side, but 16 down the other. I thought that was a bit unusual, but then I realised what had happened. He'd drawn the set wrongly on the rehearsal-room floor – which meant that all the dance-lines he'd put down were useless.

I said to Margaret Dale, the producer, 'I'm sorry to have to tell you this, but there's been a slight mishap. All those lines, they're all actually wrong.'

There was terrible consternation and after a great conference Margaret said, 'Well, there's no point in trying to transfer them. When we get in the studio, you'll just have to mark it all out again from scratch.'

No wonder that poor chap had gone sick. But because plans have never been a mystery to me – I've always liked geometry – my only thought was, 'Oh, bliss, I can do this.'

VIC GARDINER *Cameraman*
One of the biggest ballet productions Joan Kemp-Welch did was *Laudes Evangelii*, based on fourteenth-century devotional music, choreographed by Massine and with the Italian cast.

When the set was up, Lloyd Williams, the executive producer, decided to invite everybody into the studio, including the canteen staff, and he had the Bishop of London bless us before we started rehearsals.

MICHAEL YATES *Designer*
The scenery was 30 feet high, instead of the average 10 feet or so. So we were able to stage this enormous crucifixion scene, based on the original Massine church ballet.

We had Massine himself over. All right, he was getting on a bit by that time, but he was a big person, very important. You couldn't mess around with him. But Joan had him running around after her, with instructions like, 'Maestro, you must have a look at this' ... 'Now come on, Leonide, over here now' ... 'Come and stand here, Leonide' ... Nothing daunts her.

JOAN KEMP-WELCH *Producer*
One of the cameramen was Vic Gardiner, who later became a top executive of London Weekend, and I remember him doing the most wonderful track-back from Christ's face on the cross, coming right back across the whole studio.

VIC GARDINER
The actor who played the part of Christ was Pietro Angeli. While he was up on the cross during rehearsal, the cast started an industrial dispute because they heard they were going to have to pay Italian income tax as well as English. ... So he climbed down off the cross and joined them.

MICHAEL YATES *Designer*
But to take a production of that size, with that amount of dancing, and make something of it in one day's rehearsal, it was extraordinary.

A similar triumph was scored by *The Immortal Swan*, Patricia Foy's 1956 biography of Pavlova. I have now been rendered incapable of hearing the name Pavlova without recalling Eric Maschwitz's story about the only occasion he saw her dance – as she sank to the floor in the swan's death throes, one of those clear Edinburgh voices said, 'Aye, she's awfu' like Mrs

Pietro Angeli as Christ in *Laudes Evangelii*

Wishart' – but Paddy Foy's production deserves a mention here on two counts. Not only did it surmount the difficult task of combining ballet and drama convincingly, but Rosemary Gill's memory of it leads us towards another favourite topic of live television reminiscences.

ROSEMARY GILL *Assistant Floor Manager*
We used two studios on that enormous ballet-drama and all the people in it had to age as they went through their lives, but this being live television we had to change the make-up, the sets, everything, stick beards on while it was all going on, it was crazy. I remember Dennis Price, he got the giggles it was so fast and mad.

And Paddy Foy had this wicked shorthand called 'Don't you remember?' It meant anything she'd only just thought of but wasn't going to say so. Alicia Markova was dancing this enormous part, and what with the pressure and it all being live, she got pretty edgy. During a rehearsal of one of her dances from *Giselle*, she suddenly stopped and said, 'How can you expect me to

Alicia Markova

dance Giselle with artificial flowers? Where are the real roses?'

Paddy turned to me and said, 'Yes, where are they? I asked for real roses. Don't you remember?'

Well, that came right out of the blue. All very well, but ... it was a Sunday. I thought, 'Now what am I going to do?' I wandered into the property store, thinking maybe there was somewhere I could telephone, or perhaps find somebody to go to some obscure street-market. Because, clearly, this rehearsal was not going to proceed without real roses.

You won't believe it, but there in the store were a dozen boxes of real roses. The props man said they were for a play that was coming in the next day.

'Some mistake,' I said. 'Those are mine.'

I can see Paddy's face now when I said, 'A dozen boxes of roses – a gross. Will that be enough?'

Practically everyone who worked in live television has a 'props' story to tell. For those unfamiliar with the term, a prop (short for property) is any movable object inside a set.

With the exception of the clothing worn by the actors, every-thing else on display within the fixed scenery – furniture, carpets, table-lamps, pictures, books, food – they have all been supplied by the Props Department.

In those days, items which helped emphasise the set's period and atmosphere were known as 'setting-props' and these would be requested by the designer. The producer's PA, later the AFM, would also be responsible for a 'prop list', this one requesting objects particularly specified by the script, as well as any 'hand-props' – artefacts which actors handled, or dropped.

It should now be clear why there is such an abundance of props stories. Every prop provided three possible candidates for human fallibility: the person ordering it, the person sup-plying it and the person using it. To give one example of each:

FRANK HOLLAND *Assistant Property Master*
> I would always vet the property requirement forms that came in, to see if there were any doubtful items.
>
> I remember phoning once and saying, 'Iris,' I said, 'I've got your property list here. It asks for "One fur rug thrown higher from Pinewood." Now, how high do you want me to throw the rug and whereabouts in Pinewood do you want me to throw it from?'
>
> What should have been transcribed, of course, was:
>> One fur rug
>> Throne
>> Hire from Pinewood.

STEWART MARSHALL *Designer*
> In the days when we were still very punctilious about keeping any form of advertising off the screen – it's a bit more relaxed now – I received from Props one day a packet of breakfast-cereal which had been amended with a black felt-tipped pen to read 'Ellog's Orn Lakes'.

MIKE SCOTT *Director*
> When I was directing *Shadow Squad*, there was one episode about a man falsely accused of murder and its

plot was so totally absurd that the chances of the show going wrong on live television were a hundred to one.

There was a corpse who'd been found shot in a locked first-floor room. The revolver that killed him was to be discovered outside in the grounds afterwards. The heroes would prove the innocence of the wrongly accused man by demonstrating that it was all a macabre plot devised by the dead man, who had actually committed suicide. To prove this, they re-enacted a scene showing how the revolver with which he shot himself had been attached to a long piece of elastic which he'd pulled in through the window. As he fell to the ground, the revolver would drop out of his dying hand and the taut elastic would swoosh it out through the window to land outside in the undergrowth.

On every rehearsal of this re-enactment, the revolver, far from going through the window, hit the walls of the sets, hit the bookcase, or soared up into the lighting grid. It went everywhere but out through the window. We tried and tried and in the end we said, 'We'll just have to chance our luck.'

Incredibly, on air, that revolver sped straight through the window. But instead of dropping neatly to the ground it continued on at high velocity and tore a hole in the cyclorama cloth, exposing the brick wall behind. We just rolled the end credits as fast as we could.

The business of obtaining props was further complicated by the need to master a terminology that was often less than exact and lines of demarcation that were rarely precise. I can recall hearing about a drama set in Napoleonic times whose set had to include 'a writing-desk of the period, furnished with quill-pens and a few French letters'.

A note came back from the Props Department, saying that if the last item meant correspondence they could supply it. If not, it was the responsibility of the Costume Department.

FRANK HOLLAND *Assistant Property Master*

And there were costume demarcations, too. If an actress was wearing a brooch, that made it jewellery, therefore

Frank Holland (*left*) and property master Bill King (*right*) try out the first ever smoke machine used in BBC TV, in 1955

'costume'. But if it was laying on a table for a while, then it became a prop.

JOHN LANE *Floor Manager*
The first thing you had to make clear was whether a prop had to be 'fully practical'. Otherwise, if you asked for something like 'six earthworms' you might get plastic earthworms.

FRANK HOLLAND

We were responsible for practical animals, provided they didn't have to perform a trick or any other unusual thing. If it was a performing animal it would come under 'Artists Contracts'. If you had chickens running at the back of the garden, they were a prop. If, on command, the chickens all had to walk in a straight line, that was Artists Contracts.

JOHN LANE

There was 'fully practical', 'practical' and 'non-practical'. As an example in electrical terms, you could be asked to get a practical light, which meant it could be switched on and off by an actor. Non-practical meant it was just set-dressing and not to be illuminated.

There were funny combinations of 'fully practical', or not ... 'One fully practical fern,' for instance.

I was a director with *Play School* and went up north to do a photo-story for a Good Friday edition, and one of the vital props was a bunch of catkins to be on a table at tea-time, to illustrate a very moody Good Friday poem.

The AFM just put down 'catkins' on the prop list. I was short of time and was travelling from Euston for this photo-call up north, and when the catkins arrived fifteen minutes before the taxi which came to collect me, I could not believe my eyes. Props had diligently cut every single catkin off the branches, and put them in a 3 inch by 3 inch plastic bag.

I said to the AFM, 'I need catkins *on a branch*! The train leaves Euston in forty-five minutes. Get them.' Two minutes before the train pulled out she came panting along the platform with a bunch of catkins ...

CYNTHIA FELGATE *Assistant Floor Manager*

Sometimes the simplest things were the hardest to get. You learned very early on that it could be easier to get hold of an elephant for your studio than to get a 2 lb bag of sugar.

That may be the wisest observation ever made about props. Not that all the tales we heard about them were of a rueful nature. Several people's props stories recalled moments to be looked back on with relish.

w. 'bill' hillman *Property Buyer*
One of the most unusual and quite by sheer luck the most satisfying prop I had to find was Barkis's cart, for a production of *David Copperfield*. Stephen Bundy was the designer, and I said to him, 'I think I will hie me up to Beccles or somewhere in Suffolk for a couple of days and try and find this cart.'

Eventually I met up with a character who said, 'I know where there's one.' It belonged to a local saddler, who'd got it out of a pigsty in the middle of the marshes, on the fen. I found this saddler, who spoke with the most unintelligible Suffolk accent I have ever heard.

Eventually he said he'd show me the cart if I drove him there, out into this hinterland on the fen. And there was this beautiful old cart in almost perfect nick except for the dirt, and I said: 'That's it, I want it,' and I gave him £10 for it.

I didn't buy the horse, but that cart was used throughout the whole production in the Barkis scenes, and then it served in various guises – with scenery cut out on the side as a London bus, with rush and cane, all sorts of things ... till it finally went the way of all props.

frank holland *Assistant Property Master*
Viewers were always asking to buy chairs and furnishings. 'We would like to have that when you've finished with it.' And we started fashions, too. At one time we used an awful lot of Bristol-patterned cups and saucers, and as a fashion it caught on.

By the same token, some of them were always looking to see if you'd made any mistakes in period furnishings and props. But I tell you one area none of the viewing public could ever challenge you on: futuristic. Nobody could ever say, 'That was wrong'.

Also, if you had to go way, way back into the past

you'd be very unlucky to be challenged. But in-between there was always an expert looking in.

W. 'BILL' HILLMAN *Property Buyer*
Very early on after the resumption of the service in the forties we started building up the property stock and I bought a Louis XVI gilt suite – a settee and two arm-chairs.

That suite is still going strong. During the time I was there it appeared so often I don't think there's an original piece of gilt left. It's been refurbished over and over, and I've seen it on the box time and time again.

RICHARD LEVIN *Designer*
Impossible things were asked for all the time. We had a nativity play, but as sheep don't lamb at Christmas we had to fly one from Israel.

CYNTHIA FELGATE
The Steptoe sets were amazing to do props for. That's when I first learned you took photographs of sets.

When I used to make out the Steptoe prop list I had this old typewriter in the office – not that I type very well – and one week the script called for a clothes line for 'Wilfred's and Harry's underwear in the yard'.

What I found I'd typed was – 'One line full of dirty old men's underwear.' I looked at it and thought: I've got that round the wrong way somewhere.

RICHARD LEVIN
There was a very naïve children's producer, a lady who'd better remain nameless; she once sent a requisi-tion asking for a map of Great Britain showing the distribution of tits.

On another occasion, this same producer had asked Jack Kine for a special-effects weather-cock. For some reason, Props sent just an ordinary weather-cock and when it appeared her voice came over the talkback to the studio loud and clear, 'That's not the cock I asked for. It's Jack Kine's I want.'

MICHAEL MILLS *Producer*

It was at Lime Grove in Studio G and it was a very, very big show, with a lot of sets and props to be rushed in and out of the studio. The movement of properties turned out to be even heavier than we had expected, so an extra prop man was brought down from AP.

As the previous property people had been working for two days it was not deemed right that this person be allowed to bring props in and set them where they were supposed to go because he didn't know the routine. He was only deemed fit to take things out.

In the middle of the show there was a scene from *Jill Darling*, an orchard scene with swings and everything pretty-pretty, with Ian Carmichael and the chorus doing a musical number called 'I'm on a Seesaw' . . . . During this scene a previous set was being dismantled nearby for removal – remember we were transmitting live – and they said to this extra prop man who had never worked in Studio G before, 'Take the two candelabra out of the studio.'

So he looked round for an exit door, saw one, and walked straight towards it – right into the orchard set. At that moment, the music struck up and all the cast in full evening-dress launched into 'You throw me up and you throw me down' . . . and he's standing there in the middle of the orchard, in a brown coat holding two candelabra, everyone dancing round him.

For ten or twelve seconds he was stock-still looking horrified, then he bolted. After the show, I said to a lot of people, 'Well, did you see the brown coat with the candelabra?' and they all said, 'No.'

FRANK HOLLAND *Assistant Property Master*

In Props, we used to abbreviate things quite a lot. It's a quick way to communicate. If on a prop list we had got a selection of crockery I would put in brackets 'h.b.s.' - ('has been selected'), so the prop man doing the show could go to the 'Selected' shelves in the prop store.

'd.w.s.' was 'designer will select' and there were all sorts of other abbreviations. One day a chap from the

Gas Board got on to me and said, 'You've got about twenty-five of our gas cookers at Lime Grove. What are you doing with them?'

I said: 'You're joking,' because we didn't do that amount of shows needing gas cookers. I said to the props chap at Lime Grove, 'Have you got any gas cookers there?'

He said, 'Yes, we've got about twenty-five, and we'd like to know when we're supposed to send them back. They're clearly marked "n.t.g.b." – which was our abbreviation for "not to go back".'

I said, 'You bloody fool, that's North Thames Gas Board.'

BOB SERVICE *Engineer*

We were doing one of those thriller spy things – *Crane* or something like that – and we had a story all about counterfeit guineas being flooded into the country. There was one scene where all these guineas were in a safe in the wall, and the actor was supposed to be Austrian and he had to say, 'Get the guin-ess out of the safe,' which he kept saying with this phoney accent. So on the run-through the props boys actually put a bottle of Guinness in the safe, and when he opened the safe that was him corpsed for a while.

FRANK HOLLAND *Assistant Property Master*

I had a very good secretary, Freda, and I used to say, 'Freda, if anybody rings up calling for anything, doesn't matter if it's for a programme that day or the next day, tell them the boys are working on it right now.'

And John Goss, who in those days was a PA in Light Entertainment working on *Ask Pickles*, once rang to ask how we were getting on with 'Item 8'. Freda replied, 'It's all right, John, the boys are working on it right now.'

To which John replied, 'This I must see. I'm on my way down.' Something in his voice tipped Freda off, so she took the property list down and looked up Item 8. Of course, it was a mis-type. Instead of reading 'One drape', the 'd' had gone missing.

Frank Holland (*right*) and George Lazenby in a corner of BBC TV
Property Store at Television Centre

Few people have been more closely involved with television
props than Frank Holland, who joined the BBC in 1938 as a
fourteen-year-old pageboy. ('Fifteen shillings a week, plus
dress allowance, and we had to turn up at Broadcasting House
at 9 a.m. dressed in a navy blue serge suit, white shirt with a

stiff collar, nothing protruding from the top pocket and no pattern on your shoes.') Soon after he joined television, he moved into the Props Department and eventually became its head.

FRANK HOLLAND

When I took over in the fifties, producers still called every item of furniture by the name of the show it was originally purchased for, or had been mainly used in. You had the Joan Gilbert chair, the Eric Robinson music stand, the Algernon Blackwood chair. But when you got somebody new on the staff and you said to him, 'Get me the Joan Gilbert chair,' he was likely to say, 'I've never done that show, which one is it?' So I decided I'd better give all the furniture numbers.

Which he proceeded to do. He numbered every single item of furniture in the BBC store, photographed each piece and still has all those photographs in an enormous album.

His other major contribution to popular culture has been to note any odd or unusual items found in property plots down the years. Traditionally, these have helped adorn the menus of the annual prop buyers' dinners, but we have been permitted to pillage a small selection – all guaranteed to be genuine requests.

Four live husky dogs, able to pull a sledge. (If live husky dogs not available, four stuffed dogs in pulling position.)

One hydrogen bomb, non-practical.

One puddle of water, on castors.

One dead cow, with a tomahawk buried in its skull. (Should have a pleasant expression on its face so as not to frighten children.)

One well-used woman's dressing-gown.

One 3-foot by 3-foot by 6-foot deep hole.

One chicken with acting experience.

One defectory table.

One barrel of beer – pale type with nobody in it.

One bible, to be the size of a penguin.

One Gordon Blue cookery book.

Three dozen apple turnovers, uncooked. Must look like dumplings or female breasts.

One roll-up cobweb.

One live ferret – tame and toothless as it has to be handled by Bernard Miles.

One pally ass.

One large bowel for sugar.

One 6-foot ladder 12-foot long.

6 Documentaries, Informational Programmes and Commercials

Tomorrow's World was doing a documentary on Barnard, the heart man, and we had sent out for a Chinese take-away for the break, because the programme was going out very late at night, live. It didn't arrive and they were all going mad, so in desperation I peered out into the corridor where I saw two oriental gentlemen walking towards me. So I dashed up and said, 'Are you the food for *Tomorrow's World*?'

One of them replied, 'No, I'm the Prime Minister of Singapore.'

JOAN MARSDEN *Floor Manager*

Flicking through my own memories of the stuff we used to watch in those early years, I was struck by how much of it seemed to consist of people on the screen explaining things to us. Archaeology, bee-keeping, cookery, dancing – one could continue alphabetically all the way through to *Zoo Man* without exhausting the subjects on which television sages spent time instructing us, encouraging us, warning us or simply keeping us posted. (It was George Cansdale, in case anyone is still four lines back trying to remember the Zoo Man's name.) But out of all those preliminary rumblings of what was to become the Information Explosion, our most acceptable moments of enlightenment came by way of documentary programmes.

The techniques employed by documentaries have become fairly familiar these days – 'When you're a public figure,' a public figure recently confided to me, 'few things in life are more depressing than coming home to find a *World In Action* team parked on your doorstep' – but at that time it was a form that was still excitedly exploring its own possibilities. In this it had the good fortune to be served by some of the most gifted producers around, a roster that included such people as Robert Barr, Norman Swallow, Colin Morris, Denis Mitchell, Gilchrist Calder and our next contributor.

RICHARD CAWSTON *Producer*

Makers of documentary programmes have a different approach from makers of current affairs or other types of factual programmes. They are writing an article; we are writing a book. It's got to be accurate and it's got to stand up to scrutiny – for one thing, you have to persuade all sorts of people to take part and subject themselves to your editing process. So you have to build up trust.

And remember, in those days the documentary would be the main event of the evening. It was what everybody in the commuter trains would be talking about next morning. The public weren't exposed to as much information as they are today, which made subject-matter important. We kept trying to do something which hadn't been done and every year there were less subjects that hadn't been done. We were continually pushing out frontiers.

Few people pushed out more frontiers than Richard Cawston himself. His seventy-minute *This Is The BBC* (1960) was the first documentary of that length to be made without a word of commentary; *Royal Family* (1969) brought us a remarkably informal portrait of the royals as individuals; and until he made *The Lawyers* (1961) barristers had not been allowed to appear on television.

RICHARD CAWSTON

We had to get a special dispensation from the Bar Council. Kenneth Adam, who was then Controller of Programmes, gave this dinner at Lime Grove to a group of QCs and senior lawyers, led by Gerald Gardiner. I was very much in awe of them but Kenneth Adam asked

Filming during *Royal Family*: film cameraman, Peter Bartlett; sound recordist, Peter Edwards

A scene from the documentary *The Lawyers*

me to speak at the end of the dinner, to tell them why we thought we should do the programme and why they should take part in it.

Later on, a very elderly QC said to me, 'I thought you put your case very well, Mr Cawston.'

In 1961, Cawston was among the first to take documentary advantage of the newly introduced big jets which were large enough to carry 500 kilos of film equipment. That extra load-capacity enabled him to tackle the subject of *TV And The World*, in which he surveyed 20 countries in 10 weeks and went back to 9 of them for the programme. An earlier association with travel had involved him in strenuous overnight editing sessions of Wynford Vaughan-Thomas's 1949 attempt to fly round the world in eight days.

CHARLES DE JAEGER *Film Cameraman*

Philip Dorté's briefing to me for filming *Round The World In Eight Days* was: 'Shoot Wynford eating, sleeping, brushing his teeth, even being airsick – providing he is and you're not.'

Well, I lost seven kilos on that trip. I never got any food. Every time they stopped off – like in Rome, where there was a luscious meal – I had to film Wynford eating and by the time I'd filmed it, it was time to get aboard again. And that's what happened everywhere.

When we got to Honolulu I took some shots of Wynford with hula-hula girls dancing round him and he said, 'Charles, for heaven's sake, see that doesn't get into the film. My wife wouldn't be very amused.'

So when we got back I asked Dick Cawston, our editor, not to include that bit of film, and he made sure it went into the throw-out bin. As luck would have it, the *Sunday Mirror* rang up a few days later and asked our film manager, Jack Mewett, if he could help them. They wanted to print some pictures from the *Round The World* film. Jack went down to the cutting-room and rummaged around in the bin where he knew there'd be some throw-out pictures and just happened to take out that particular bit of film.

So there, the following weekend, right across the Sunday paper, was a big picture of Wynford and those hula-hula girls.

Round the World in Eight Days: Wynford Vaughan-Thomas (*left*) and cameraman Charles de Jaeger arriving in Australia

It was an era when many sensibilities still bruised easily. 'How long must we suffer the disturbing spectacle of over-exposed female legs on *TV Dancing Club*?' complained a viewer in 1955, and the following issue of the same magazine had another offended customer asking, 'Why must fighters be shown spitting into bowls during boxing matches?' Nor was this sensitivity confined to the receiving end of the cameras. Among those in charge of programmes, cheeks could just as easily be set aflame.

STEPHEN HEARST *Producer*

Nothing could show the change in the moral climate of television better than what happened with a documentary I made about Mayfair in 1953.

To show one aspect of Mayfair – the highly organised prostitution that was going on there then – I did a shot of a pair of high-heeled ladies' shoes in close-up on the pavement. They were joined by a pair of men's shoes; then you saw the four shoes going out of frame.

After the programme had been transmitted I had a note from Cecil McGivern, the Controller of Programmes, saying he thought it wasn't good enough: that shot just wouldn't do. I should remember we were in the family entertainment business.

Remember, nothing was said in the shot. There were just the two pairs of shoes . . .

ANDREW MILLER-JONES *Producer*

In a documentary called *Her Infinite Variety*, about women's changing shape, there was a segment arguing that the whole art of dressmaking was to deceive the eye, and this was demonstrated with historical drawings and classical paintings of naked women.

When I explained the programme to Norman Collins, he said, 'But you can't show a naked woman!'

'But it's art,' I said – and he said, 'Even if it's art, there must be a balustrade in front.'

However delicate other people's susceptibilities may have been, the only factual programmes likely to make me avert my eyes from the screen in those days were the ones dealing with medical matters. Nor, it seems, was I the only victim of what might be termed 'Viewer's Flinch'.

JOHN LANE *Floor Manager*

In one of the medical programmes there was a kidney bowl full of a human brain, or it might have been half

a human brain. It was terribly vital, though, and had to
be in the studio at a certain point. So I went to the prop
man and said, 'Right, this has got to be brought in at that
point in the script.'

I turned away to talk to somebody else and when I
turned back I couldn't see the prop man anywhere. He
was on the floor, in a dead faint.

ANDREW MILLER-JONES *Producer*
In my series *Matters of Life and Death* in 1950 dealing
with surgical procedures we were going to use a piece of
film from an actual operation. What it showed was about
four square inches of stomach, a nice neat cut, needles
going in, and so forth. It ran less than five minutes and
there wasn't enough blood to fill a thimble.

But the girl whose operation it had been wrote in via
her solicitor saying that she hadn't minded sacrificing
her modesty in the cause of science when she had been
filmed in hospital, but she was not going to allow herself
to be shown on television.

My reply was that if any of her friends could recognise
her from four square inches of her stomach, all I could
say was she was no better than she should have been.

HUGH TOSH *Photographer*
A friend of mine was watching an early medical programme about an appendix operation, where the first
thing they did was show a piece of rubber stretched over
a box, to demonstrate what was going to happen. When
they cut through the rubber, my friend passed out.

Despite the reaction of Mr Tosh's friend, it was found that
most viewers were fascinated by such hitherto closely
guarded secrets of the operating-room. As a consequence,
there was a time in the early fifties when, as someone pointed
out, so many medical documentaries were being aired that the
quickest way to get to see a doctor was to switch on your
television set.

The trend probably began in 1947 with *I Want To Be A
Doctor*; but it was not until 1958, with Richard Cawston's *On*

Call To A Nation, that the medical profession agreed to become involved in a programme that included frank criticism. Prior to that, their relationship with television can be illustrated by one of Andrew Miller-Jones's experiences.

ANDREW MILLER-JONES *Producer*
In the course of that *Matters of Life and Death* series, early in the fifties I was going to show a surgical operation being performed by Sir Hedley Atkins, who ultimately became Professor of Surgery at Guy's. At this time, though, he was at a critical stage in his career and Sir Heneage Ogilvy, another distinguished surgeon who was presenting the programme, said to me, 'I don't mind my name being mentioned, the GMC can't do anything to me, but Hedley must wear his surgical mask so that he can't be recognised, and you must also put some "distort" on his voice. It's such a jealous profession that, otherwise, when his name comes up for promotion they'll say, "Oh yes, that chap who was seeking publicity on television" – and that would be the end of that.'

Although TV never managed to breed a Television Doctor to match the popular Radio Doctor, it did come up with 'regulars' in other specialised fields of information-mongering. One of the most unexpectedly successful of these was General Sir Brian Horrocks, who lectured on great battles of the past with engaging fervour. He was equally well-liked by people behind the camera, especially his Floor Manager, Joan Marsden, known to all who worked with her as 'Mum'.

JOAN MARSDEN *Floor Manager*
He was Black Rod then, an important official in the House of Lords, and he would never use autocue. He used to learn his script off by heart, after he'd had it typed in his office in that larger than normal type. It always said in the top corner, 'Black Rod, House of Lords'; then under that, 'Wait for cue from Mum'.

MICHAEL BOND *Cameraman*
General Horrocks always looked on the studio as a military thing, so he gave everybody ranks. The senior cameraman would be sergeant major and the lieutenant would be in the gallery, and the tracker would be a corporal or whatever, so it was fixed in his mind what the hierarchy was.

Lieutenant General Sir Brian Horrocks

ROSEMARY GILL *Producer's Assistant*
I remember David Attenborough's first time on telly. I think he was a trainee producer at the time, and I believe it was before *Zoo Quest*. But I can remember saying to him, 'If you don't mind me saying so, you can't go on television like that, your hair is all sticking up,' and I lent him my comb. I think his hair has stuck up ever since so it was a bit of a waste of time.

PAMELA PYER *Photo Clerk*
When I went into the studio for the first of Patrick Moore's *Sky At Night* programmes, I expected to see all

sorts of electronic marvels. In those days, its opening titles took the viewer through a window to the twinkling stars beyond. I saw the window-frame in a corner of the studio, with a huge blow-up of the night-sky behind it, so I said to the cameraman, 'How do you make the stars twinkle?'

'I just wobble the camera a bit.'

SHEELAGH REES *Producer's Assistant*
We used to like the cookery people best – we could go down from the gallery and eat afterwards.

A lovely lady called Joan Robbins cooked by gas and Philip Harben did it by electricity. I remember he put the food in the oven once, opened the oven door later on and said, 'Well, they're not quite ready yet. Goodbye everybody.'

Afterwards S. E. Reynolds, the producer, said to him, 'Why did you sign off? I could have given you a few more minutes.'

Harben said, 'It wouldn't have done any good, I forgot to switch on the oven.'

Cookery programmes were very much a feature of afternoon television, whose contents were often tailored so slavishly to what were then considered to be the preoccupations of housewives and their children that Eric Maschwitz dubbed it 'The Opiate of the Mrs'.

ROSEMARY GILL *Producer's Assistant*
On one of the afternoon programmes we had a scientist who had been brought in as an expert on detergents. He was quite extraordinarily nervous, poor man, and he stood up and said, 'Good afternoon, I am going to talk to you about washing –' then he fainted.

And the cameraman, from sheer force of habit, panned his falling body all the way down to the floor.

JIM POPLE *Director*

We had a one-hour afternoon programme in the early Rediffusion days that fell into two parts. The first half was a children's magazine programme, directed by one director, and in the second half was a children's drama serial, done by another director. The problem was that they both took place live in the same studio, so you had to literally change over during the commercial break. Within the space of less than three minutes, one director and his PA had to slide out of their seats in the gallery, the director for the serial with his PA slid in, and all the cameras had to rush down to their marks at the other end of the studio.

There was one occasion when I was directing the magazine half and we had a heron in the studio for one of the items. It's a big bird, the heron, and this one got away and flew up into the lighting-grid area where nobody could get him down.

Well, this being live we couldn't stop for it, so, comes the second half, off they go into the drama serial with the bird still up there.

Somewhere in the middle of the serial, the heron moved and sat on a hot lamp, which gave it such a surprise that it fell off and descended in a cloud of feathers into the set of somebody's living-room. It landed behind a settee, and while the camera was off that part of the set, a scene-hand hurled himself behind the settee and collapsed on the heron. For the rest of the story there was much unexplained noises off and throbbing of wings.

ALAN PROTHEROE *Reporter, Wales*

We used to do a daily magazine programme with one camera in a tiny broom-cupboard of a studio where we had four guys sitting in a row. One was doing a review of the religious week in Wales; one was doing a countryman spot and had a sheepdog under his chair – because you couldn't pan the camera downwards nobody ever saw the sheepdog, but you could hear him; a third man was doing a report on something else; and the fourth was doing 'What the Papers Say' long before Granada took up the idea.

The system was, I always introduced the guy on my immediate left, and the camera would pan to him. When he finished, the camera came back to me, and this man on my left would get up and tiptoe down the end of the line, and they'd all move up one. Another guy would now be next to me, I'd cue him, and so on.

One day, I made the fatal mistake of introducing the guy three along first, instead of the one next to me. So there was this terribly slow, seemingly endless camera pan from me down a line of genially smiling faces, none of whom I had introduced, until the camera finally reached the man at the end of the line. And then, of course, after his piece came the slow, endless pan back to me . . .

MICHAEL BOND *Cameraman*

There was an afternoon series with Baron, the photographer, where I had someone with me who'd never tracked a camera before. Baron always used to put on a rather cultured voice when he was addressing the camera, but on one occasion this chap tracking me kept

The photographer Baron

panning me down and down on to the table Baron was working on till the camera hit it and it started splintering. And we suddenly heard Baron say, 'Oh, gorblimey, the table's going up!'

Possibly because this type of actuality programme made less use of celebrities and show-business notables than most other television departments, those who did pay a visit tended to linger in the memory.

JIM POPLE *Film Editor*
When the film *Around The World In Eighty Days* went out, *This Week* had Mike Todd in for an interview – it wasn't simply a political series in those days, it had some jolly stories as well. There was also a West Country bishop on the programme and he asked Mike Todd for an autograph for his daughter. Mike Todd pulled out his cheque book, wrote out a cheque for a million dollars, signed it and gave it to the bishop – presumably in the certain knowledge that a bishop would never try to cash it. Or that, if he did, the bank was bound to query it.

ANDREW MILLER-JONES
I had Sir Alexander Fleming on one programme and we showed the petri dish with the original penicillin culture in it. And he said to me, 'I will go down in history as the man who made it possible for a soldier to have gonorrhoea twice in the same week.'

MICHAEL LATHAM *Editor*
It was soon after the first-ever heart transplant and a colleague of mine at the time, Peter Bruce, persuaded Dr Christiaan Barnard to come to the UK to do a *Man Alive* programme. He flew in from America, arriving at Heathrow at about 10 a.m., and every single newspaper – and, more importantly, both our own BBC TV news and ITN – had sent reporters and film crews to cover his arrival. Drastic action was needed if we weren't to lose our scoop. If we didn't get him away from the airport fast, the whole impact of our programme the following evening on BBC 1 would be lost.
After a council of war, we discovered that the only thing allowed to park at that time on the tarmac at

London airport was a hearse. Before anyone realised what was happening we'd got hold of one and whisked Barnard away into the airport tunnel. The second part of the plan was for two cars to follow right behind the hearse and stop in the middle of the tunnel so that no one could get past – thus enabling Barnard to make a quick, safe getaway and then go into hiding. And that's what happened.

It took four or five hours for BBC TV News to discover where the intrepid *Man Alive* team had hidden Barnard, by which time he was giving us an in-depth interview.

JOAN MARSDEN *Floor Manager*

On one of the *Apollo* programmes, a children's *Apollo* 'live', and terribly difficult to rehearse, we had James Burke and Patrick Moore answering children's questions. Princess Anne was being shown round the studios and she came in during one of the rehearsals, accompanied by Huw Wheldon. 'Now tell me about the moon,' she said to Patrick.

Well, you know Patrick. An hour later, or so it seemed, he was still explaining about the moon. Up in the gallery they became more and more agitated. There was the director and the overall *Apollo* programme director up there and I had them, and others, yelling at me on headphones. 'Think of a way of telling her she's got to go' ... 'Get her out' ... 'Use your loaf'.

Eventually, I went up to Huw Wheldon, and I just said, 'I'm afraid we do actually have to rehearse now.'

Stunned silence ... 'Well, all right,' he said, 'We'll go.'

Her detective fell about, and she sort of pulled one of those, you know, 'faces' – appreciating that even princesses can be ordered out of rehearsals.

ALAN RICHARDSON *Film Recording Manager*

When Brigitte Bardot arrived to appear in a *Highlight* item, every engineer and technician seemed to have something to do in the corridors, checking cables and so on. As we walked through Lime Grove, we had to push our way to get into Studio P.

The interviewer, Geoffrey Johnson Smith, asked her if she had any pets. She said she had a pet dog and a pet monkey, adding – in her rather French way – 'He's very naughty really, he goes pee-pee all over the flat.'

There was a serious top-level conference afterwards about whether this line of dialogue should be allowed to go out.

From that moment onwards Studio P was always known as Studio PP.

Studio PP Lime Grove

Highlight was a ten-minute early-evening programme whose budget has been variously estimated as 'About £25' or 'About £30'. Produced by Donald Baverstock and using three interviewers, Cliff Michelmore, Geoffrey Johnson Smith and Derek Hart, it was the seed-bed for the most stylish and influential topical programme of its time – *Tonight*. If *Panorama* brought to television an equivalent of the front-page story, *Tonight* provided the inside-page, gossip-column and cartoon.

ALASDAIR MILNE *Deputy Editor* Tonight

We wanted to 'cut the cant', as we used to say. A slice of life every night. There would be serious topics, but we also looked for eccentric items: the man from Bristol with a bent egg was a famous one; and the lady who saw fairies at the bottom of the garden. (Cliff asked her what colour they were, what size, and so on.)

We recruited from the recently folded *Picture Post* Gordon Watkins, Cynthia Judah, Trevor Philpot and Fyfe Robertson – an extraordinary character with his hats, and so good at telling a yarn, able to do long five-minute set-pieces straight to the camera.

With Tony Jay we invented writing verse to accompany film, something he had an extraordinary gift for. When Beeching's axe fell, Tony wrote a marvellously nostalgic piece that brought in all the railway station names.

When we put Alan Whicker on, it was his TV debut. His very first story was about some Oxford Street traders. Yes, it was OK. But then he did one with some Ramsgate landladies which demonstrated how cheeky he could be, and after that he never looked back.

With those new recruits, led by Donald Baverstock – clever, widely read, with a brilliant flair for the topical story – plus our *Highlight* team of presenters, including Mac Hastings, we were away . . .

MIKE SCOTT *Producer*

I had said to Granada in 1956 I wouldn't mind going on the screen myself. They said, in the kindest possible way, 'Sorry, you have a speech impediment, you can't pronounce your 'r's.'

At that time, the 'in' voice was a rather standard BBC voice; then Cliff Michelmore and *Tonight* came along, setting a style of casualness and willingness to be fallible which struck off a lot of shackles. It also meant that my rather poor 'r's, unacceptable in 1956, were acceptable by 1963.

Tonight. (*Left to right*) Cliff Michelmore, Derek Hart, Cynthia Judah, Anthony Jay, Fyfe Robertson, Peter Batty, Gordon Watkins, 'Slim' Hewitt, Donald Baverstock, Alasdair Milne, Barbera Vesey-Brown, Alan Whicker, Geoffrey Johnson Smith

The *Tonight* team in conference in Studio M, Kensington

ALASDAIR MILNE *Deputy Editor* Tonight
Our breakdown technique became famous. We were constantly ringing Cliff on air to tell him to 'go to Birmingham, Bristol isn't ready yet', or 'get Alex to sing a song', or 'forget about the film, Tony says he can't finish it for another ten minutes'.

Cliff didn't rely on autocue, just cards with his stuff written on, so as we made changes he'd have to shuffle his cards and alter his running order in vision.

But that was his particular genius and part of the spontaneity of the programme. When *Tonight* was in trouble everybody watching knew it ...

POLLY ELWES Tonight *Reporter*
Six months after *Tonight* started, Donald Baverstock asked me to be their first woman reporter. One film story I recall was about sheep on Ilkley Moor getting into back gardens and eating the chrysanthemums, because the moor wasn't fenced. We did a recce and there were the sheep, loads of them, doing just that.

The next morning we came back to film it and there wasn't a sheep to be seen. So everyone – the cameraman, the director, the engineer – we went up to the moors, found some sheep, drove them down and put them into people's gardens.

Whether the subject of commercials follows logically from a story about herding sheep is a question that calls for fairly thoughtful evasion. But shortly after eight o'clock on the night of 22 September 1955 – it was, of all unimpressive days, a Thursday – an estimated two million screens displayed a picture of a Gibbs SR toothpaste tube encased in a block of ice; and suddenly our television world was filled with scented soaps, tinned beans, mature ladies in crossover bras, and a delightful man who emerged from a small tent on a sunlit hillside to tell us, 'There's no pleasure like rolling your own.' Almost overnight we learned that margarine should be pronounced with a hard 'g', armpits should be called 'underarm', and distinctions ought to be observed between 'fast relief', 'fast, fast relief' and 'express relief'.

Certain television staff, however, greeted the new development rather in the way my mother used to accept any new labour-saving device: 'Something else to go wrong.'

Gibbs SR

STEVE WADE *Director*

Dreadful things happened with live commercials. In one that we did for a brand of stuffing, the chef presenting it had to turn to the oven, open the door, and produce a beautifully cooked chicken. Unfortunately, he took so long about everything that the commercial over-ran its time, so Presentation cut him before he opened the oven door.

All hell broke loose, especially from the clients who'd come along to the studio to watch their commercial being transmitted. Out came their stop-watches, there was a bloody row and finally, because they spent a lot of money with us, it was agreed we could do the whole thing again.

This time the chef managed to get through the commercial on time. The only trouble was, nobody had told the scene-hands we were doing it again. When he opened the door to get the chicken, all he brought out was a skeleton. They'd eaten it.

For a while, in ITV's earliest days, another vehicle for transmitting live commercials was a curious hybrid called the advertising magazine, or 'admag'. This odd form of entertainment-substitute, a blend of soap-opera and selling, generally consisted of a collection of garden-suburb characters mixing gossip and news about each other with earnest claims for various consumer articles they happened to find on their persons.

JIM POPLE *Director*

There were some near misses, particularly with *Jim's Inn*. As one had to do things live, you either had to ever so slightly fix them, or hope for the best.

There was one occasion when somebody's adhesive for sticking tiles on bathroom walls gave dear Jimmy Hanley a problem.

The idea was, you spread the adhesive on the back of the tile and just pressed it to the wall, and there it was, permanently fixed. When Jimmy started to take his hand away he could feel the tile slipping, so he hastily put it back on the tile, ad-libbing like mad all the while about this marvellous glue. Then he took his hand off again and the tile started to slip again, so we cut away rather quickly to something else. As we did, Jim took his hand off and plain as anything you heard the sound of a tile slithering down the wall.

DAVID WILSON *Managing Director, Southern TV*

Admags were very good. They were a way of getting advertisers, without it being too expensive for them. But oh ... we used to have terrible troubles with them. Things going wrong.

When the first non-drip paint came on the market,

one particular character had to demonstrate how this paint never dripped. He got so carried away with what he was saying, he rammed a huge paint brush into a great pot of paint ... Rammed it up to the hilt in the paint while he spoke into camera, enthusing about the wonders of this paint that never dripped.

As he picked up this huge paint brush it was going flop ... flop – all over the studio floor. Nobody could stop him. Flop ... flop ... And it was going out live, you see. Flop ... flop – our lovely non-drip paint!

STEVE WADE *Director, ATV*

In an admag called *Fancy That*, Noelle Gordon was the presenter and our chief customer, who shall be nameless, was a splendid man who made furniture. He brought his wonderful 'bargain of the month' furniture along, and when we went into the studio Nolly took one haughty look at it and said: 'I wouldn't have it as a gift.'

I said, 'Right, that's the way we'll start. Then we'll have Mr Nameless in to defend his furniture.'

Within a week he'd sold the whole perishing lot.

JIM POPLE *Director*

We once had to have somebody show a cream caramel, but the trouble was once you made one and put it into the studio it promptly sank under the heat into a messy-looking goo. So we literally had one of them made with starch. Rock solid, but I think a justifiable cheat.

SYLVIA PETERS *Presenter*

I was in a lot of advertising magazines for Southern TV – the way we made them reminded me of the early days of Ally Pally – and I did a lot of ads for kippers.

Many months later, I was walking along near my home and a woman looked at me, stopped me, and exclaimed, 'Christ'. Then she said, 'I'm sorry. But as soon as I saw you I remembered I'd forgotten the fish.'

Some would claim – always a sneaky way of side-stepping 'I would claim' – that if there is any nostalgia mileage at all in vanished commercials, it resides in their 'jingles', the catchy little songs featured by some of them. It is certainly true that the potency of jingles was established quite early in the game.

CLIFF ADAMS *Musician*

In the fifties I had a group called The Stargazers, who were extremely well known, and the first jingle we were asked to sing was for Murray Mints: 'Murray Mints, Murray Mints, the too good to hurry mints.'

It was one of the earliest commercials and our voices were behind a cartoon involving soldiers – a soldier in a bearskin being called by his sergeant major and saying, 'I'm sorry, you'll have to wait, I'm finishing my Murray Mint, the too good to hurry mint.' Then we went into the jingle.

Well, the greatest accolade at that time for a pop group – or 'vocal group' as they were called then – was to do the Palladium. We achieved that about three months after commercial television started but there were a lot

Murray Mints

of recording artists on the same bill so we were in a dilemma about what number to do.

We took a big chance and ended our act on what we called 'our latest recording'. We actually came on in bearskins and re-enacted the commercial on the stage at the Palladium. Then we pulled off the bearskins and inside them we had packets of Murray Mints which we threw to the audience. It caused a sensation, and showed the power commercials had, even within three months.

Cliff Adams went on to become a successful composer of jingles himself, responsible for such imperishables as 'For mash read Smash', 'And all because the lady loves Milk Tray', as well as the much-acclaimed melody for Fry's Turkish Delight.

The acknowledged king of the jingle, though, was Johnny Johnston, who led another popular vocal group, The Keynotes. He was the thirty-second Mozart who had us humming 'I'm going well, I'm going Shell', 'Softness is a thing called Comfort', 'A Double Diamond works wonders', 'Hands that

Johnny Johnston's 'Shell' jingle

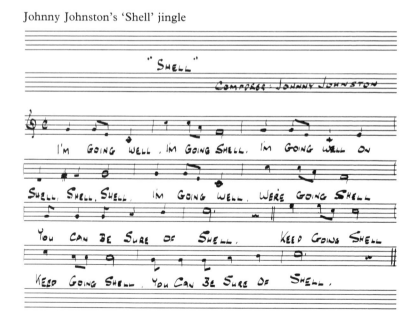

do dishes can be soft as your face', 'A Thousand and One cleans a big, big carpet (for less than half a crown)', as well as my own favourite example of fitting the melody to the words, 'Save, save, save, with the Co-Operative Permanent Building Society'.

JOHNNY JOHNSTON *Composer*
The first jingle I did was for Bournvita. It was very simple. The tune went 'Sleep sweeter Bournvita' ... which was repeated ... then there was a yawn and 'goodnight'. It was one where I did the singing myself; and, do you know, my mother, who was getting on a bit, would never go to bed until she'd heard me sing it. It ran for ages but it didn't matter how tired she was, she'd wait up for me to sing 'goodnight'.

CLIFF ADAMS *Composer*
One notable jingle I wrote was for a cigarette called Strand and the commercial was called 'The Lonely Man'. There was this actor, Terence Brooks, who looked like Frank Sinatra, standing on a street in London, wearing a trench coat, with a hat on the back of his head, stopping to light a cigarette. Then this theme came on. As soon as the commercial went on the air, enquiries started coming in, people ringing up and asking if there was a record of the music available. So obviously I went in a studio very quickly, made a record and called it 'The Lonely Man Theme'. There was no vocal, there was nothing mentioned about cigarettes, just the musical theme.
It had been out about ten days and had had about four broadcasts when to my consternation the *News Chronicle* came out with a half-page headed 'Auntie BBC plugs Cigarette'. Straight away, that very day, the record was banned from the BBC.

CHRIS SHARPE *Graphics Designer*
That campaign 'You're never alone with a Strand' – when you look back now, it was hysterical. It was a slogan everybody knew but nobody wanted to buy the

product. All the viewers took out of it was that you're always *alone* with a Strand; they thought the character was some sort of mackintoshed poof, skulking around the back streets. So it flopped.

JOHNNY JOHNSTON *Composer*

For 'Beanz Meanz Heinz' the kids came from the Children's Home in Harpenden, Herts, and from the Arts Educational School. There were eight or ten of them, plus two or three of my girls, and the kids loved coming down. If we were nearly through by, say, half-past eleven they would come up to me and say 'Can't you drag it out? If we don't finish till half-past twelve we can have lunch in your canteen and we won't have to go back to school till three o'clock.'

CLIFF ADAMS *Composer*

The length of a so-called 30-second commercial is actually only 28 seconds, for various technical reasons. Well, I was once commissioned to do a piece of music that started with about 4 seconds of vocal and finished with 4 seconds of vocal - what we call 'top-and-tail' – and in the middle 20 seconds just orchestral music, over which we were later going to record a commentary. So we recorded the musical part - the top and tail vocal and the orchestral bit for the middle – made sure it ran 28 seconds, and left it till a commentator was booked.

When we got one, I went into the recording studio again with the pre-recorded 28-second music tape, played it and cued the commentator to come in after the first vocal. He said his piece, in came the end vocal and that was that. I thought it sounded first-class.

But there was a young, enthusiastic man there from the advertising agency and he said, 'Could we do one more take, please?'

So we went through it again, in came the commentator over the 20 seconds of recorded orchestral music, end vocal – again it all sounded fine. But again, this agency man wanted to try another take. This went on about four or five times, until I finally said, 'Can you tell me what's wrong?'

He said, 'I'm trying to get one at exactly the correct timing.'

I couldn't believe it. He was sitting there with a stop-watch, obviously pressing it either too soon or too late, because he was making every single take come out a different time. He simply hadn't grasped that he was timing a piece of pre-recorded tape.

JOHNNY JOHNSTON

It was Christmas-time and I wanted to buy my wife a little Mini. I'd gone to Luton to collect it but we got into a terrible fog and though I'd arranged to meet a man called Harry Raelbrook at two o'clock, I didn't get back till about four o'clock, and he was still sitting there smoking his pipe. I'd never heard of him before because this was the start of his business, so I apologised and he said, 'I want to advertise on television and I want a jingle. I make shirts.'

I said, 'What's special about your shirts?'

He said, 'You don't have to iron them.'

So I sat at the piano in my office in Denmark Street and played and sang these seven words – 'Raelbrook

Toplin, the shirt you don't iron.' I repeated them three times and then again in a changed key, and I said, 'Something like that?'

He said, 'That's what I want, don't change anything.' We never did.

That rare kind of moment was not confined to the musical side of making commercials. There were elements of the unexpected for everybody involved.

ROGER ADAMS *Producer*

We were filming a commercial for Triumph Herald outside the Royal Albert Hall, and, to illustrate its all-round independent suspension, it began with a girl walking down the steps and a driver in a Triumph Herald following her down them. That worked fine, but as the car was doing this, the maintenance foreman in charge came rushing out saying, 'You've got to stop. There's a garage underneath and you're bringing the ceiling down.'

Well, the rest of the commercial's plot was this: the car follows the girl, and when the driver sees her meet her boyfriend he puts the car in reverse and it goes back up the Albert Hall steps.

The way we were going to show it doing that was by reversing film of the car coming down the steps. But now we were under pressure from this foreman, who kept shouting, 'You've got to stop.' So the stunt driver simply put the car in reverse and tried driving that Triumph Herald back up the Albert Hall steps.

The car did exactly what the makers said it would.

PETER BOSTOCK *Copywriter*

In the early days we were producing a commercial for Mackeson's and it consisted of people doing a thumbs-up sign. They found a lovely old farmer down in the West Country, got the film team down there and he said his bit and they said, 'Now give us the thumbs up.' Out came his hand and – something nobody had noticed – his thumb had been chopped off in a threshing machine years earlier.

CHRIS SHARPE *Graphics Designer*
I worked on 'People Love Players', a big TV campaign in those days. It was very romantic and soppy, and it ended, 'I kept the packet to mark the day.' We always rather enjoyed that because we thought we could double it up with the London Rubber Company.

DAVID WILSON *Managing Director, Southern TV*
When the ITCA became so insistent on truth in advertising they challenged us as to whether one of the detergents really did make something whiter than something else. At that time our Controller of Advertising was Graham Dowson, a marvellous man who had no inhibitions. He solemnly had great piles of laundry done in one detergent and some in another, then for a whole afternoon he himself stood out in Regent Street stopping everybody as they passed saying: 'Is this whiter than this?'

CHRIS SHARPE *Graphics Designer*
I worked on the launch of Hartley's New Jam. That was in the black-and-white days and it was fun because it was at the time of year when there weren't any strawberries – in those days they didn't come in from Israel. So we had to cut out some black-and-white photographs of strawberries and drop those into the jar.

SIMON THEOBALDS *Reporter*
We have always in the south been able to split commercials on separate sides of the Region. In those early days a manufacturer of sausages had bought only one side of the Region. And he was so concerned that all should go smoothly he himself cooked the sausages in the studio.
Very sadly, when the commercial was transmitted, sound and vision somehow got crossed with a COI food hygiene filler on the other side of the Region.
So the pictures of the sausages went out with a food

hygiene message about the importance of keeping your
food clean. But on the other commercial you saw pictures
of flies crawling over rotting meat and heard a voice-
over saying how delicious so-and-so's sausages were. I
don't know what the sausage man took us to the cleaners
for. He's never been back.

BILL PODMORE *Cameraman*
We had Maria Callas making her first television appearance one night and I remember everybody being in a
panic about her, because she had this reputation of being
the tigress of Milan. But Jenny, the make-up girl, told
me that when she was making her up, Callas said, 'What
time is it?'

Jenny said, 'It's Chocolate Time' – that being the
catchphrase of a commercial that was very big then.

Callas said, 'What is-a this "Chocolate Time"?', so
Jenny explained. By then it was getting a bit late, and her
husband came in very anxious, saying, 'Maria, Maria,
do you know what time it is?'

'Yes, I do know,' she said. 'Chocolate Time.'

7 'Semi-live': Film, Telerecording and Videotape

Forty Persians had been hired to play the Berber tribesmen in a production of *Beau Geste*. At the end of the day's filming, we gave them small tubs of cleansing oil for removing their make-up. Six make-up girls stood open-mouthed when they proceeded to drink it.

SALLY ANN BRAGG *Make-up Supervisor*

In the forties and fifties there was a widely held conviction that live television possessed a unique kind of integrity. In an article Derek Burrell-Davis wrote for the 1957 *TV Annual* about his popular *Saturday Night Out* programmes, he declared, 'We never cheated you with film and we never will. We believe it will always mean more to you, the viewer, if you can believe that what you see is actually happening now.' Even the head of the BBC Film Department, Philip Dorté, stated in a 1955 interview that, 'Television should have as little film as possible. Pre-filming would take out all those little human touches which the viewer watches with sympathy to see how the victim gets out of the slip.'

That endearing faith in the intrinsic virtue of live television may have been encouraged by the fact that filming in those days, with its heavy and cumbersome 35 mm equipment, was an uncertain and laborious process. (Even the phrase the BBC used for it then – 'film effort' – seemed to have overtones of panting and gasping.) Nevertheless, producers in live drama and Light Entertainment did make occasional use of filmed 'inserts' – sequences shot in advance, either to set the scene or to give actors time to change costume or dash over to another part of the set; while a proportion of filmed material was also essential, as we have seen in previous chapters, to newsreels, current affairs programmes and documentaries. One way or another, even the earliest live television went in for a certain amount of film.

ANDREW MILLER-JONES *Producer*
> Pre-war, because all the film boys had to work in dark-rooms without any light at all, the BBC gave them an extra pint of milk a day for their health.

MICHAEL MILLS *Producer, Light Entertainment*
> Back in 1949, when I did *Choir Practice* written by Cliff Gordon, I created a great stir because I actually went out and filmed something for its opening, to be shown under the title. I shot a lady getting on a train at Paddington, and I bribed the engine-driver to make a great cloud of steam as the train pulled out to block out the camera. We mixed to the sky, panned down – and there we were in a South Wales station where the same lady got off the train and walked up the street. It may not sound much now, but at the time it was a sensation.

STEPHEN HEARST *Director*
> The first four programmes the then young and glamorous Chris Chataway did for the BBC in 1956 were called *Away From It All*, using that great heavy synchronised-sound film camera. For one of the programmes, we went to Wales to look at slate being quarried. When this huge monster was angled a certain way – to forty-five degrees – it started to make a terrible noise. The quarrying involved an explosive blast every hour. In the end we put the camera right into the middle of the quarry in the hope it would get blown up.

ALAN RICHARDSON *Film Recording Manager*
> Philip Dorté, the first Head of Film Department, had this lovely nonchalant approach to life, and he always smoked a cigarette in a long holder which gave him immense panache. He was walking through to the projection room one day to go and see a film, and it so

The early film camera used in *Away From It All*

happened we'd just moved over from 1,000 ft rolls of film to 2,000 ft rolls, quite big and heavy. Now, if those rolls weren't wound reasonably tightly, the middle could fall out – and in the Film Department that was reckoned the cardinal sin, rather like the chap who sneezed at Trooping the Colour.

Philip was standing beneath the iron staircase that went up to the projection room and the projectionist was either nervous or rushed, because he was holding the roll of film horizontally, which is bad anyway, because you should always hold it vertically. Then, as luck would have it, the centre did fall out and all the unwinding film went straight down onto Philip Dorté.

He was literally encased in a cone of film with the top of his head and his cigarette holder poking miraculously through it. This was flammable film, so if he'd had his cigarette alight, he'd have gone up whoof!

To transmit such rolls of film on television, they have to go through a specialised projection machine called 'telecine', operated at a distance by technicians who maintain constant loudspeaker communication with the control gallery. In my experience, they are selected for total unflappability and a curiously uninflected voice quality.

ROS POOL *Producer's Secretary*

You could stop and start telecine from the gallery. I worked on one play with Lance Seiveking just after the war and we'd got a piece of film of traffic going round Piccadilly Circus. Lance said, 'Stop,' so we stopped it.

Then he started it again, stopped it, then he said, 'Oh, I do like this effect. It makes me feel like God.'

CYRIL WILKINS *Technical Assistant*

I was once in pre-war AP days asked to take over in telecine when someone was off. There was a film loop going round and they said, 'Watch this and if you see the film break for goodness sake stop the machine and put the shutter down, otherwise the film will catch fire.' So I was watching this loop – it was Madeleine Carroll singing some song or other – and then sure enough one of the splices in the film started to open up. So I shut it down, got the film out, took it to the room at the back, spliced it, put it back and tried to restart the machine.

Now, this was a Baird machine, designed by John Logie Baird, with two or three motors on it, and I couldn't get it going properly at all. All the while the transmitter engineers were bleating because they were not getting anything but I wasn't getting anywhere. Then a chap with glasses wandered in, so I said to him, 'Do you know anything about these things?'

'Oh no, laddy,' he said, 'I only designed it. I don't know how to run it.'

John Logie Baird

JIM POPLE *Film Editor*

As film editor on *This Week* I found they were trying to be topical even then, but being topical with 35 mm film and separate sound-track was not easy. Once I was still editing part two while part one was going out on the air, and I missed a join. It actually hammered its way through telecine with a paper clip holding it together instead of film cement. It was hailed as quite an achievement.

BRIAN TESLER *Director*

When I was with ABC Television we put out a film called *The Thief of Bagdad*, an Alexander Korda film with Conrad Veidt. The reels got mixed up and they played the final reel before the penultimate reel, so that it went Reels 1, 2, 4 and 3.

There wasn't one phone-call. It got a very high rating.

Because there were still difficulties in matching studio picture-quality to that of a film-camera, 'inserts' rarely went unnoticed by viewers. Whenever the television screen leapt suddenly into dazzling brightness or faded for no reason to a muddy grey, people all over the country would nudge each other and say, 'That's a filmed bit.' (Is there any other activity, with the exception of sex, that promotes such expertise among non-professionals?)

RICKY BRIGGS *Film Cameraman*
We were filming a sequence for *No Hiding Place* in a street down by the Embankment, a scene of three police-men pursuing the villain, whom we'd already filmed disappearing down the Underground. Now we were shooting the three coppers chasing after him: specific-ally, two uniformed men and Mike McStay. If you remember, he and Johnny Briggs used to play Super-intendent Lockhart's side-kicks.

Well, just as the three of them were pelting past the camera, with the plain-clothed Mike in the lead, a gentle-man passing by saw this scene of what appeared to be a man running away from two uniformed constables. So, those being the days when the public were encouraged to 'have a go', this chap stepped forward and fetched Mike one smartly across the head with his silver-knobbed cane.

They had to take poor Mike to Charing Cross hospital.

SYBIL HARPER *Production Assistant*
I did my PA training with Hal Burton, when he was doing a serial by Vincent Tilsley called *Champion Road*, a sort of early *Coronation Street*. There were filmed inserts in each episode, and all of them were going to be shot before we started in the studio. For the opening scene we needed a small mean-looking street, so Hal sent his Floor Manager up north on a recce to find a suitable filming location. The FM came back with some photo-

graphs, and when I looked at them I said to Hal, 'But there are houses just like these round the corner in Shepherd's Bush.'

Hal said, 'But, dear, the bricks are different.'

It was my first intimation of how much attention was paid to detail.

Champion Road on film location. (*left to right*), Vi Carson, Anna Turner, William Lucas, Jack Howarth, Hal Burton, the Floor Manager, Jimmy Sainsbury assistant cameraman, James Balfour (*kneeling*), Sybil Harper

FRANK HOLLAND *Property Master*

For a Light Entertainment filming requirement, Prop Department were asked late one afternoon for a quantity of London newspapers to set up a newsvendor's stand. I said to our petty cash buyer, Jimmy Whigham, who had just got back from buying the day's perishable props, 'Go down to Shepherd's Bush tube station and buy 20 copies of the *Evening News*, 20 copies of *The Evening Standard* and 20 copies of *The Star*.'

Instead of going out of the TV Centre at the Frithville Gardens gate, he went out at the McFarlane Road exit underneath the railway arch, and when he saw a news-vendor's stand, he went up to the chap and asked for 20 copies each of *The Evening News, The Evening Standard* and *The Star.*

The newsvendor just ignored him. So Jimmy asked again, saying, 'Please, I need them for a filming session with a newsvendor.'

The chap said, 'Piss off – this is the bloody filming.'

RICKY BRIGGS *Film Cameraman*
Tanya Lieven was a brilliant director with one particu-larly endearing quality. Because she herself had only a somewhat tenuous grasp of technical matters, she placed absolute faith in the technicians she entrusted them to. Consequently, she was one of those people who some-times manage to achieve the impossible simply because they themselves never realise its impossibility.

A case in point was the occasion when she was doing a modern version of *Leda and the Swan.* I got a telephone call to go and see her at ten o'clock one morning in some rehearsal room at Kingsway. She greeted me with her customary 'Daah-ling' – then, 'Ricky, I want you to go somewhere and film a swan for me. And what I need this swan to do is come out of the water, go straight up to the camera, shake its wings in a very aggravated manner, then turn away and go back into the water.'

Well, as you can imagine, my immediate reaction was to ask her, 'Have you arranged a specially trained swan for that?' Because, of course, if she hadn't, it was the sort of shot you could spend two or three weeks trying to get.

She just shrugged and said, 'Oh no, daah-ling. I am leaving it to you.' Then she turned back and got on with her rehearsal again.

Well, because my knowledge of swans' habits and habitats is getting on for next to nothing, the only idea that came to mind was to drive over to Regent's Park. I wandered round gloomily till I came to the lake area, where I found a lot of nannies and old ladies feeding some ducks and, yes, swans.

I began to get out the camera gear, and then I noticed

a swan coming towards me on the narrow canal bit of the lake. So, as quickly as I could, I set the camera up and started running the film in case the swan might decide to come out of the water and forage for some crumbs.

Well, it did come out of the water. What's more, it walked towards the camera and not only ruffled its wings in high dudgeon, but then – incredibly! – it turned round and went straight back into the water. I had the whole thing – first time, and in no more than fifty-foot of film!

I jumped in the car and was back in Tanya's rehearsal room by eleven-fifteen. In high excitement, I said to her, 'You're not going to believe this, but I've got that shot!'

'Daah-ling, I knew you would. What were you worried about?'

ROS POOL *Producer's Assistant*

For *Mr Polly* we did a bit of filming on the river. It was my job to stay on one river-bank and whenever we were about to shoot, I had to ask all the courting couples to remain hidden in the grass.

Every ten minutes the lock gates would open, all the motor boats would come up and as soon as they'd gone, the director would shout across at me, 'Make them all lie down.' And I'd go running up and down the bank saying, 'Do you mind just keeping down?'

ROSEMARY GILL

I remember one film sequence for *The Railway Children* when I was an AFM; as luck would have it the way the planning schedules worked out meant the film had to be shot in deepest winter.

I can see those children now, in their summer dresses. I had gone out with a hammer and screwdriver and scraped all the snow away, knocked holes in the earth and planted some plastic daffodils. And there they all gambolled about in summer dresses. It was very lyrical, but I have never been so cold, and when we got to the end of the shoot the littlest one was in tears because she was so perished.

ELIZABETH AGOMBAR *Costume Designer*

There was a six-week children's serial directed by Rudolph Cartier about a schoolgirl who won a dress-design competition. Of course, the dress had to be rather special, so I designed one and the actress playing the schoolgirl was to wear it in a pre-filmed scene.

I don't remember the exact sequence of events, but the dress was delivered to the actress's home after the filming. It was left in a box in the entrance to the flats where she lived, and it got stolen.

I raced back to Conduit Street where I'd bought the material, but there was none of it left, they'd sold out and weren't replacing it. If I'd have been able to get some more, I could have made the dress again and there wouldn't have been any problem. So we all sat down and said, 'What can we do?'

Somebody said, 'Why don't we put out an SOS on radio and TV, begging whoever pinched that dress to bring it back, telling them why.' So we did, and the dress was returned – it just reappeared.

RICKY BRIGGS *Film Cameraman*

For the children's serial, *Sexton Blake*, we were filming a studio scene where Sexton Blake is menaced by a full-grown Bengal tiger inside a cave. When Sexton makes a dash to escape from it, a portcullis drops down between him and the tiger, effectively stopping the beast coming after him.

The clapper-boy stood well back to mark the shot but he smacked the board down with such a hell of a bang that it must have sounded to the tiger like a rifle-shot. All I can tell you is, he took off – and his forward path being barred by that portcullis, he leapt straight over the camera ... Over the dolly, right over my head – he cleared the lot.

And not only did he clear it, he took with him the man from Chipperfield's circus who'd had him on a concealed chain. This Chipperfield lad also went soaring over the camera. And because he still didn't let go of the chain attaching him to the tiger, he was dragged on his stomach across the studio floor.

The whole thing happened in only a matter of seconds, but when I looked round, instead of the usual thirty or forty people you generally find hanging round a studio – electricians reading newspapers, props men sipping tea, and so on – the place was empty. The whole lot of them had left ground-level. They'd all shinned up the nearest walls or ladders and were now peering down at me from the overhead gantry.

JACK KINE *Visual Effects Designer*

A lot of car drivers will remember the morning the great white whale went home to his mum in the Natural History Museum. It was for a film sequence Michael Bentine dreamed up in the first series of *It's a Square World*. The whale was 40 feet long and about 15 feet

Frank Thornton (*left*) and Michael Bentine (*right*) filming for *It's a Square World*

high with 25 scene-hands walking along inside it, and a chap with a stirrup pump squirting water on its back.

We had been told that at 7 a.m. that particular morning they were re-routing the traffic because they were about to start road works, and the road we were coming along would be clear. The information was wrong. So you can imagine all the buses, taxis and private cars lining up behind this 40-foot whale. It caused one of the biggest traffic jams ever.

YVONNE LITTLEWOOD *Director*

I was quite a raw recruit when I took over *This Is Your Life*, which then used to be done by the BBC. It was around the time when they decided that the 'pick-up' – the bit where Eamonn nobbles the victim – should be a pre-filmed sequence. They would film it every Monday morning and show the processed negative film that evening. But probably because that was then such a short time for processing to be done, there'd invariably be something technically wrong with the film.

Every single week I went through agonies. For six months, I sat there in the gallery, cued the opening, on would come those shots of clouds *This Is Your Life* used to open with in those days, then I would mix through to that morning's film of the pick-up and something about it would be wrong. That six months felt like six years.

One programme I remember particularly was the week when the subject was some worthy fellow who'd come down from Leeds and Eamonn picked him up, in a great crowd of people, at Euston station. I mixed to the film of it, there was Eamonn with his mike, this gentleman gets off the train and walks along the platform, but nothing could be heard. No sound at all. I can remember yelling, 'Sound on film, where's the sound gone?' – then just babbling. I can recall thinking, 'Not again! What shall I do? Shall I just fade the whole thing out? Stop it and start again? No, that's not possible, it's live. Shall I come straight in on him on the stage? But the curtains haven't opened yet!'

In the end, as far as I can now remember, we just had

to go straight over to the stage, because with no sound on the film it was all we could do. But that was just another of our weekly disasters and somehow I got through the show.

Afterwards, I was talking to Eamonn in his dressing-room, when Jacko - T. Leslie Jackson, our producer – came in and said, 'I've had a reporter on the phone asking if I could confirm that viewers heard someone on the show blaspheming.'

I said, 'I don't remember anybody blaspheming.'

Jacko said, 'Well, I didn't think so, either. But he said that at the beginning of the show, they could hear some woman's voice saying, "Oh Christ, not again"!'

Eamonn said, 'Come to think of it, I could hear your voice all day from somewhere.'

I said, 'Now you tell me . . .'

Next morning the papers were full of it. Of course, I was terrified. I thought, 'That's it, there's going to be a row about this.' But nothing happened next day, and on Wednesday there was nothing either. When Friday came, I couldn't stand it any longer. I asked to see Mr Maschwitz, our boss, went in and there's tall Eric . . . a big cuddle and a kiss on the cheek, and, 'Hallo, how are you today, what's wrong?'

'I'm terribly worried, I don't know what to do. I thought you'd be sending for me on Tuesday.'

'What are you on about?'

I said, 'About Monday night and my voice being heard. Hasn't anybody said anything?'

'Oh that,' he said. 'Come to think of it, somebody did bring it up at Programme Review on Wednesday and I said, "Oh, go on, that was just Yvonne asking for help from above."'

That minimum two days' requirement for film processing was one of the snags in 'telerecording', an early method of recording programmes by placing a film-camera in front of the television screen. Its other drawback was the resulting

DAILY *He tu...*

SKETCH

TUESDAY, OCTOBER 31, 1961. 3d.

© 1961, by the Daily Sketch

Woman's voice in TV shock

A WOMAN'S voice shocked BBC televiewers last night.

She was heard following a breakdown at the start of "This is Your Life" programme.

Eamonn Andrews was seen talking into a microphone.

There was no sound from him but someone was heard calling "Sound on film! Sound on film!"

One word

Confusion. Then, in a woman's voice, a one word exclamation which to most viewers sounded blasphemous.

A BBC spokesman said: "A hitch, especially in a programme like 'This Is Your Life' can make people get hot and bothered."

Daily Sketch, 31 October 1961

quality which, in the discreet phrase employed by engineers of the period, 'added loss to the picture'. Consequently, it was used mainly for archive purposes or the sale of historic programmes overseas; only rarely for re-transmitting domestically.

RICHARD CAWSTON *Film Editor*
I was told that the very first telerecording ever sent abroad was of the wedding of Princess Elizabeth in 1947. The story I heard was that it was done by means of something that was known as the 'broncoscope' – because one of its principle components was the cardboard tube out of the middle of a Bronco toilet-roll.

VIC GARDINER *Cameraman*
At Rediffusion, telerecording helped us to cope with game shows like *Double Your Money* and *Take Your Pick*. It enabled us to record, say, twenty contestants and use the best five.

PADDY RUSSELL *Floor Manager*
We had this scene in the opera *Salome* at Riverside studios where everybody came pouring out of the banqueting hall and the thrones were brought out by slaves. It was critical where the thrones were set down, because the crane-camera had to come behind the rostrum and shoot down at Salome on her dance.

They never got it right. Even though there were hefty marks on the rostrum showing where they should be set down, they were never in the correct places. In the end, after the dress rehearsal, Rudolph Cartier said to me, 'There's only one answer, Paddy, you will have to go on with the slaves.'

I stood there in my slacks and sweater and said, 'Pardon?' Being Rudi, he just walked away.

I shot off to find Pam Glanville, the wardrobe mistress, and said, 'Help! I have got to have something I can wear, so I can go on with those slaves and make sure these thrones hit their marks.'

In blank astonishment, she said, 'Ah yes. Well let me have a think about that.' Of course, at Riverside, we didn't carry a store – our store was back at Lime Grove – and the only thing she could come up with was a great length of chiffon material, about 3 ft wide and 12 ft long. So we wound me in it, starting at the feet and going all the way up, with the last bit over my head to disguise my headphones. I said to Rudi: 'All right, I will go on. But for love of heaven don't get me in shot.'

Floor Manager
Paddy Russell
in costume

Now although we were doing the programme live, it was also being telerecorded – one of the earliest tele-recordings – and when, much later, we saw it back I could have killed Rudi. There was the shot of the slaves coming out of the banqueting hall carrying thrones, and following them was this self-satisfied Roman matron who picked the thrones up, set them down again, then walked off.

By the end of 1957 a newly developed method of telerecording had improved its quality sufficiently to overcome the objections to using it for transmission. But videotape recording (VTR) was soon to overtake it. The autumn of 1958 saw it being put into operation, gradually and somewhat gingerly, by both BBC and ITV.

ROGER APPLETON *Engineer*
Rediffusion were the first company to have VTR machines in 1958, but they were used at first purely as a fail-safe device. We would record a programme, then – while the recording was being transmitted – we would perform the programme again in the studio live.

The idea was that if the recording broke down, we could have gone back to a live transmission.

JOAN KEMP-WELCH *Director*
The first time Rediffusion used a VTR 'insert' in a programme was during a musical series with Dickie Valentine called *Free and Easy*.

In those days, it needed a twenty-second countdown into it, and when it worked like a dream everyone in the control gallery clapped.

DAVID WILSON *Managing Director, Southern TV*
When video recording started, my order was that it was not to be used for retakes. If ever there had to be a retake for any reason, it could only be with my permission.

Sure enough, when they were videotaping an admag, the presenter dried and expected to be allowed a retake. He hit his head and called to the deity. Everybody in the studio did everything they could to make him go on. The Floor Manager was there saying, 'Get a move on! Get a move on,' and the cameraman was saying, 'Go on, go on!'

In the end, after what seemed several minutes, he suddenly realised that he had to get on, so he picked up his lines somehow and struggled on.

They came to me afterwards and said they would have to do the whole thing again, because they couldn't edit videotape in those days. I said, 'No. You will put the whole thing out on the air as it is, as a lesson to all artists. You will bleep the cry to the deity, and you will fire the presenter.'

And that's what happened. It was about three years before we were finally driven to follow the example of the other companies and start re-taking.

One of television's true innovators has been Philip Saville, whose imaginative 1963 production of *Hamlet* at Kronborg Castle, Elsinore, to celebrate the 400th anniversary of Shakespeare's birth, was the first play to be recorded almost entirely on videotape and performed entirely on location. Scenes like the entry of the Players through an archway into the castle courtyard, where the wheels of their cart really did bump and rumble over the cobblestones, or the magnificently shot scenes on the seashore with the castle in the background, set new standards for television drama.

The cast included Christopher Plummer as Hamlet, Robert Shaw as Claudius, Michael Caine as Horatio, Roy Kinnear as a Gravedigger and Donald Sutherland as Fortinbras, while the Players included Steven Berkoff and Lindsay Kemp.

Danish Television, who first put the idea to the BBC, supplied Outside Broadcast personnel and equipment, though it was Bob Wright who suggested to Danish technicians who were holding lights above their heads that it would be less tiring if they attached them to long rods. To this day, such devices are known in Denmark as 'Boblights'.

BOB WRIGHT *Lighting Director*
I'd been working with Michael Caine about four weeks previously when he got killed off in *Dixon of Dock Green*. I was talking to him on the way back from Elsinore and

Hamlet at Elsinore
Christopher Plummer and Jo Maxwell Muller in the chapel of Kronborg
Castle

he said, 'I don't understand a word of what I'm saying.'
So I said, 'Well, why do you do it?'
He said, 'I have a feeling you get seen on this sort of
show. The right people will watch it.'

Philip Saville's *Hamlet* was billed at the time as 'live on tape', meaning that it was shot as though live. The technology for editing videotape still presented problems. Although a certain amount of editing was possible, it required physically cutting the tape with a razor-blade while peering at it through a magnifying glass, then re-joining it with a piece of silver tape, a process that would take an experienced editor ten minutes or so each time.

Sydney Newman Head of BBC Television Drama with producer Peter Luke

Of even more importance, we were constantly being told, was the fact that an edited tape could not be re-used, and as each one cost around £90 ('which was a lot of money in those days') editing had to be regarded as both a privilege and a luxury.

Electronic editing of the type used now did not come into general use until the mid-sixties, and it brought with it a complete change in the style and nature of programme-making. But until its arrival, the era of 'live on tape' was played out against the usual backdrop of enjoyable desperation.

DOUGIE HESPE *Stage Manager*
> We were recording a navy programme from the boys' training ship, *HMS Ganges*. We wanted to show what the lads could do, and one thing they could do was a Whale Boat Race just off-shore.
>
> Another Stage Manager, John Frost, was on top of the hill overlooking the race and the idea was that he would raise his handkerchief when he got the word that the recording was running, and an admiral would start the race by firing a gun.
>
> The great moment came. John Frost got the message from Scotty, the director, to 'stand by', and he raised his handkerchief. After thirty seconds Scotty said to him, 'OK, relax, they've got a technical problem back at Television Centre.'
>
> So John relaxed and lowered his arm. Bang went the gun and that year's Whale Boat Race was never recorded.

INNES LLOYD *Stage Manager*
> I was recording carols from Canterbury and the Archbishop, in the middle of his message, suddenly stopped and covered his eyes. I thought, 'Help, what's happened?', because he'd had an operation on his eyes shortly before. I rushed in and he said, 'My eyes have gone, I can't see any more!'
>
> I then had a good look, and it was a lamp that had been moved so that it was reflecting into the autocue he was reading from at such an angle that you could no longer make out the words on it. If that had been a live programme, goodness knows what we would have done.

JOAN KEMP-WELCH *Director*
> At the time when you could record things but you still couldn't edit, I did a programme called *Gala* which had

enormous publicity because in it we had Tito Gobbi, Maria Callas, Iturbi, Fistoulari, the Royal Philharmonic, Markova and a Russian dancer whose name escapes me. It was a mammoth musical evening and an evening of back-stage complete disaster.

The first thing that happened was that Fistoulari, who played 'Bolero' for this Russian to dance, had been asked not to leave the studio at the end of it but to stay there, because Iturbi was supposed to come down and join him at the grand piano, and they were going to do two pieces, a Chopin and a Liszt. But when Fistoulari heard the great applause from the audience, he left from sheer force of habit – which meant we had nothing to look at. In the gallery we were shouting, 'Send him back, send him back!' and back he came with Iturbi.

They had been told to bow to one camera and then to turn and bow to the other; whereupon they each bowed to the wrong camera and I got a great close-up of their bottoms. I quickly cut to another camera and, of course, they immediately turned and I got their bottoms again.

The next thing that happened was that Iturbi sat down at the grand piano, smiled at Fistoulari, who smiled back at him, and they both started on the wrong piece of music: one on the Chopin, the other on the Liszt. So they both stopped and waved to each other. Then the camera, trying to go round the grand piano, got stuck.

The next terrible thing was that the compère called Tito Gobbi, 'Gobi'. Gobbi was supposed to go straight into his music, but because we had a live audience and they applauded, the conductor waited. The cameraman didn't know what to do, so he went on to Gobbi, who was polishing his nails on his lapel. We cut quickly to the conductor and pressed Fistoulari's cue-light saying, 'Play, play, play!' So he promptly started, and what we got on camera was Gobbi breathing on his nails and rubbing, then looking very surprised and sweeping on.

The last disaster was with Markova, who always used to like to take the end of her dance leaping on to her partner's shoulders. We said, 'Don't do that, because the camera can't hold both you sitting on your partner's shoulders and your partner – it's too low a shot. Take just an ordinary call.'

Did she? Not on your life. So we got a picture of Markova, her legs crossed and her partner's head sticking out below them.

I was left with a videotape of this terrible programme that had all these mistakes in it. I went out with our programme controller, John McMillan, and we got tight out of sheer despair. Everybody else was eating strawberries and cream but we were just moaning on each other's shoulders. I thought, How in the world can I cover up these gaffes? Because we couldn't edit, you see.

What I did was this. On the day of transmission, I made up great arrangements of gorgeous flowers and leaves and placed them so that they looked as though they were round the studio we'd recorded *Gala* in. Then, while our recorded programme was going out, whenever we came to a mistake in it, I cut to an enormous thing of flowers, keeping the sound going, then cut back again after the mistake.

Next day we got notices saying, 'This smooth as silk programme ...' I thought, 'Little do they know.'

8 'Treasured Moments'

Everybody used to make me laugh, the Floor Managers, the cameramen, everybody in the studio. One of them used to throw nuts at me, trying to get one down my cleavage just as I said, 'Good evening'.

Sometimes he succeeded. I'm sure that's why I always looked so jolly.

SYLVIA PETERS *Announcer*

This final chapter is probably the best place to make a somewhat delicate point: namely, that however naïve and misguided early television practitioners may now appear, they were no more so than viewers of that period.

One could cite, for instance, those who wrote to tell the press how they had conducted tests proving that a TV set weighed more switched on than it did switched off. Another batch of correspondents wanted it known that a television set in a room would keep mice away, the scientific reason being that it emitted frequencies inaudible to the human ear. There was a group who claimed that a large roll of cellophane hung in front of the screen would prevent eye-strain, while others preferred warding off that hazard by placing a large bulbous magnifying glass in the same position. Frank Muir had a relation who was convinced that when she switched off a play the actors went home.

A sizeable section of the viewing population wrote to inform the BBC that their pet animals sat for so many hours in front of the television set that it proved conclusively that they could understand what they were looking at; was it not, therefore, the BBC's duty to provide special programmes for them? One lady whose cat had particularly regular viewing habits even went to the trouble of submitting a sample format, entitled *Pussy's Half-Hour*. Most of its details escape me now, but they included several close-ups of fish and bowls of cream. (Up on the fourth floor of Television Centre, we spent some pleasant hours debating who would be the most suitable producer for the programme.)

There is, then, considerable evidence that the confusions, delights and pirouettes of that era were not confined solely to one side of the screen. To those of us on the far side, however, the formative years of television – coinciding as they did with our own formative years – will always remain a special time of our lives. But as no useful purpose is served by going all puffy-eyed about it, we decided to round off with this assorted collection of memories.

ROYSTON MORLEY *Producer*

I was invited to lunch with Sir John Reith at his house in Beaconsfield. It was a jolly good lunch and with the fish I was asked whether I would like a glass of white wine and with the steak would I like a glass of red wine? I accepted both, although I noticed that the other six or eight people there were all drinking water.

After lunch I was shown into the library and while I was inspecting the fine collection of books his voice behind me said, 'Mr Morley, I see you are a drinking man.'

SYBIL CAVE *Production Secretary*

At Lime Grove, we often had visitors in the gallery watching what went on during a drama production. This was at the time when plays still had an interval in the middle and, during one interval, Royston Morley said to me, 'Take the visitors down and let them have a look at the studio.'

The visitors on this occasion were David Oistrakh and Khachaturian. They each took one of my hands, and I'll never forget walking between them, hand in hand.

MICHAEL MILLS *Producer*

One great break-through moment came when we moved to Lime Grove from the cramped conditions of Alexandra Palace.

I did the first programme from Studio G there, and I made the compère, Bill Fraser, drive on in a sports car – just to show we had the room!

BINNIE MARCUS *Producer's Assistant*
We were recording an *International Concert Hall* with Paul Tortelier, the cellist. After the interval, he entered and went up on the platform, the audience applauding as he sat down. They quietened as Colin Davis, the conductor, looked at him for a signal to start. But Tortellier seemed to be fidgeting a bit, then suddenly he got off his chair, propped his cello against it and crouched down on the platform, moving his hands around.

That caused quite a bit of rustling among the audience, so Antony Craxton, the producer, asked the Stage Manager to find out what was wrong. The next thing we saw was the SM also on his hands and knees. When Colin Davis joined them, the audience began to laugh and Antony had to stop the recording.

Via the SM's headphones, he asked Tortellier, 'What's the matter? Can I help?'

Tortellier looked up and said, 'I'm so soorey, but I've lost ze 'ole.'

The podium had been turned round during the interval, and we eventually had to get all hands on deck to rediscover the hole for his cello.

IAN ORR-EWING *Outside Broadcast Assistant*
For a time we tried out a colourful character called Colonel Brand as a tennis commentator. He was delivering one of his quick-fire commentaries – 'Smash, recovery, smash, recovery' – when he suddenly said, 'Oh, my God, it's gone hurtling into the Royal Box toque-high.'

Well, everybody knew Queen Mary used to watch from there and as that was the kind of hat she was renowned for wearing, the BBC received any number of complaining calls. 'Was it our habit to refer to Her Majesty's headgear in this light-hearted way?' We had to put out an apology.

PAUL FOX *Editor*
About two weeks before one of the space shots, Dick Francis was in the NBC studios in New York because

he was directing something for the American Election. In the middle of this election programme some fellow phones him up and says, 'Dick, I know you're busy, but I can let you have 30,000 feet of early space film, all excellent material.'

Well, Dick used to talk space language a lot in those days and when the guy started to press him – 'Do you want it, Dick?' – he very firmly said, 'Negative' and put the phone down.

A week later he received 30,000 feet of negative film.

CHARLES DE JAEGER *Film Cameraman*
When we did a series about ancient Greece with Sir Compton Mackenzie, we went out and filmed some Greek countryside scenes, brought the film back, and had it back-projected in the studio behind him while he was talking to the television camera.

Unfortunately, in one of the scenes you could see a motorcar passing through, which looked all wrong for the subject-matter. So what did we do? I tied a long piece of string to Sir Compton Mackenzie's foot and the moment the car appeared on the back-projected scene behind him, I gave the string a sharp tug. Whereupon, he turned around and said, 'Ah, but in these modern days ...'

JOAN MARSDEN *Floor Manager*
It was Guy Fawkes' night on a *Blue Peter* programme, and we had all sorts of fireworks around the studio. The director said to me over talkback, 'Right, Joan, cue the Catherine-wheel.'

I did, and it was lit and went whizzing round. It was all happening. Then I heard on my headphones – 'Right, Joan, cue the Catherine-wheel to stop.'

PETER MORLEY *Director*
In the late fifties I directed a live discussion programme for Associated–Rediffusion called *Conflict*, with Wolf Mankowicz and one other guest where the idea was to discuss a certain topic knowing the two of them would basically disagree on it. Came a week when the subject

Spike Milligan

was 'Comedy' and the guest Spike Milligan.

The opening music started over a studio silhouette shot and with fifteen seconds to go, Spike leapt out of his chair, went behind a cameraman and bit him on the ear. So the programme opened to shrieks of unseen laughter. The opening caption ended and there was Spike walking onto the set tucking his shirt into his trousers and doing up his flies.

Near the end of the programme, two cameras were released to shoot the closing captions. The lights went down leaving Spike and Wolf in silhouette again, Spike leapt out of his chair and asked the Floor Manager for a piece of chalk – then, as the first caption was super-imposed over the silhouette, a large hand came into shot. It was, of course, Spike who had walked over to the caption to chalk a huge exclamation mark on it. The next caption, shot by the other camera, read 'Editor: Cyril Bennett'. Over that he had now chalked '9 out of 10'. The third caption was printed 'Directed by Peter Morley'. The chalk message said, 'WHO HE?'

ROGER ADAMS *Producer*
We used a farmer in Kent called Bob Todd in a Schweppes Shandy commercial. We shot at Camber Sands, where he had to be buried up to his neck in sand because he was supposed to be in the desert and suddenly the beer is put before his eyes but it gets whipped away before he can quench his thirst.

It took ages to dig a hole large enough for a man to stand up in, but finally Bob was 'buried'. We did a couple of takes and then it came on to rain. As it was lunch-time we all went over to the beach hut, where we had lamb chops, but – with Bob's agreement – we left him with an umbrella stuck over him.

While we had lunch, we kept an eye on him because it was really entertaining to watch people walking past, not really looking, then they'd hear a voice say, 'Good morning'. And when they looked for the source of the voice, they saw this head in the sand ...

SYBIL HARPER *Production Assistant*
After a *Come Dancing* programme, I had to get details of one tune Edmundo Ros's band had played, so I asked Edmundo about it and he gave me the title, which I forget now, and said the composer's name was Eros.

Well, all that kind of information was sent along to the Performing Rights Society, for them to work out who got what in the way of royalty payments, so you had to make certain you had all the detail right. And because I'd never heard of a composer called Eros, I checked the name with BBC Music Library, who said they couldn't trace him either.

So, just to be sure, I rang Edmundo's office and his

secretary said, 'Oh, yes, that's one of his own composi-
tions.' ... Of course – E. Ros.

INNES LLOYD *Assistant Presentation*
Kenneth Milne-Buckley, T. Leslie Jackson and myself
once invented a chap called 'Gaston de Wolfe, CBE',
whose position in the BBC we put down as 'S.ex.Tel'.
(Could be read as 'Senior executive, Television'.) We
gave him an office and we used to send him memos, with
cross-memos to other people.

To go with him we invented a piece of equipment
called the 'Litvic' machine, a sort of cousin to a television device called 'Genlock'. It was a 'self-phasing
AC/DC-operated telecine camera' and we used to book
it for programmes. We did actually write to Cecil
Madden, the Programme Controller, saying we thought
we really should buy one of these machines for our-
selves. He of course said, 'How much?' and when we said
'£300', Madden said, 'Go ahead and buy it.'

I can't remember the consequences of that, but I
know we eventually had to retire Gaston de Wolfe, CBE.
We succeeded in getting his retirement recorded in
Ariel, the BBC house-magazine. 'After distinguished
service with the BBC for many years,' etc. – the usual
sort of thing for anyone at that high executive level.

JANE SCRASE-DICKINS Costume Designer
There was a day when Harry Belafonte was walking
through a scene dock at Lime Grove to get to one of the
studios and he saw an upright piano, stopped, and
started to play. People just moved in and within ten
minutes there must have been about three hundred
people standing around him. Not a word spoken. Just an
old piano stuck up in the scene dock which Harry Belafonte happened to find. A marvellous moment. It was
magic.

CHARLES BEARD *Fireman, Wood Green Empire*
I had a big black Alsatian I used to take on duty with
me, especially when I was on nights, with the Teddy
boys about.

'Duke' his name was. He came from the air force and he could put out lighted cigarettes, matches, bits of paper – anything that was burning. Some he'd put out with his paws, some with his mouth – slobber it all, till it was put out.

Frank Beale said to me, 'I don't see why he shouldn't have a meal allowance.' So we saw the management and they allowed me £1.50 out of petty cash for food for him.

FRANK HOLLAND *Design Clerk*
After I was demobbed I went to see Peter Bax, who was then called 'Design Director', and he said, 'Good morning, young lad, it's nice to have you back. Did you have a good war?' Then he said to me, 'What's your ambition?'

Well, I'd just returned from the army as a young, cocky sergeant, about twenty-three or four, so I said, 'To be quite honest, I'd like to sit on the other side of the desk where you're sitting' ... never realising that many years later that's what I'd be doing. I inherited it from Peter Bax, and I sat at that desk till I retired in 1984.

BOB SERVICE *Cameraman*
A cameraman's 'cards', the ones he has clipped to his camera during a production, are his life-blood, especially in something like an hour-and-a-half play. They contain his cues and instructions about where he has to be, where he's got to move to, what lens is needed and so on. He's completely lost without them.

There was one cameraman who used to wait till a colleague was away having a coffee break then he'd substitute the man's cue-cards with another set. When the chap returned from his break, this cameraman would pick a row with him, then in pretended rage, pluck the cards off his camera and tear them up.

PETER DIMMOCK *Assistant Head, Outside Broadcasts*
Back around early 1955, I wrote a memo saying that we've always been the poor relation at Broadcasting House, but now that ITV is coming and we're going to have a competitor, why don't we get some recognition

by changing *Radio Times* to *Radio and TV Times*?

'Oh, my dear chap, that's being much too commercial,' I was told.

Then along came ITV and – what made me hopping mad – there was *TV Times*.

ROS POOL *Producer's Secretary*

The first programme I ever did was *Cradle Song* with Harold Clayton producing. I was working on it within a week of going to Alexandra Palace, and I hadn't even seen television. Harold would say, 'Do so and so, darling,' and I wouldn't pay any attention. He'd have to say 'Miss Pool', and I'd spring to attention. The crew all fell about, but I didn't know he meant me.

NORMA GILBERT *Television Press Officer*

Every year there were a series of major press conferences to announce the autumn and winter programmes. At one of Sydney Newman's drama conferences, with all the national and provincial TV writers present, a question came up about a new play, *Cathy Come Home*, by Jeremy Sandford, which was similar in style to *Up The Junction* by Nell Dunn. Both plays – *Cathy*, concerned with homelessness, and *Up The Junction*, with back-street abortion – were controversial.

Leonard Marsland Gander, the doyen of TV correspondents, said to Sydney, 'What do you call this kind of play? It's not a play and it's not a documentary.'

Sydney Newman replied, 'I suggest you call it "agitational contemporaneity".'

The following Sunday two leading Sunday paper TV writers, Philip Purser and Maurice Wiggin, accused Sydney of butchering the English language. In his Monday *Daily Telegraph* column Leonard Gander reported that he had looked up the word 'contemporaneity' and discovered that it was first used in the nineteenth century by, of all fortunate names, Cardinal Newman.

DEREK BURRELL-DAVIS *Producer*
For one circus programme at Ipswich I had a full-size reproduction made of a TV camera. It was so realistic that when our boys arrived, they said, 'What – five cameras today?' On the final rehearsal, when the clowns were using it in a mock explosion sketch, they accidentally blew it up.

Which left me with bits of the dummy camera scattered all round the ring and no time to replace it. I was at my wit's end. But when the audience were let in, who should be the first person to arrive but the local craftsman who'd made it. As a matter of course we'd given him a free ticket to the show and he'd decided to use it. By the time the show started, he'd put all the bits and pieces together again as good as new.

MARY CREWE *Production Assistant*
We were in Denmark filming and we went out from Copenhagen on the train to Elsinore. I couldn't resist putting on the expenses, 'Taxi from Elsinore to outlying hamlet'.

TREVOR HILL *Producer*
It was the hot summer of 1956, with studio lights even hotter. I'd been summoned from Manchester to Lime Grove – a new boy working in Children's TV – to produce, among other things, a programme with Mary Malcolm and some Rover Scouts demonstrating new equipment for camping.

Mary was wearing a sun dress with a bolero. Before transmission she was so warm she took off the bolero. Because I was busy setting up my closing shot of a camp fire with scouts in silhouette round it, I didn't notice this until we were on-air.

The second the programme ended, Freda Lingstrom, in charge of children's television then, was on the phone. She could be lavish with messages of praise, known in the department as 'peppermints'. I was expecting a peppermint, but no: she had seen on the screen a head and shoulders shot of a naked woman! I got a terrific rocket and the worst of it was, I didn't even know what I had done.

DEREK HARPER *Sound Engineer*

When I was covering President Eisenhower's tour of Asia, I found on arrival in Delhi from Rome that the box with our microphones was missing.

There was no television in India at the time so I arranged to borrow a microphone from All-India Radio. I went to collect it and met the senior engineer. He handed over the microphone but made me promise to bring it back first thing next morning. He said, 'You must bring it back ... Otherwise, All-India Radio is off the air.'

GEORGE CAMPEY *Television Publicity Officer*

There is a classic broadcasting expenses story told of René Cutforth, a brilliant war reporter and broadcaster. As part of his expenses sheet he regularly put in expenses for entertaining 'Count Ludendorf', a Polish diplomat.

For ages, René's expenses came in regularly with 'To entertaining Count Ludendorf', until one day an accountant suddenly said, 'I think this chap is dead. He died about three years ago.'

So a message was duly sent to René that it was believed Count Ludendorf had been dead for three years; would he explain why this name came up regularly on his expenses?

Back came a message, 'Am investigating.' Then eventually they got a signal: 'You are quite right. Count Ludendorf was killed three years ago. I have now discovered I have been entertaining an impostor.'

CYNTHIA FELGATE *Floor Manager*

The first week I went on *That Was The Week*, one of the senior scene-hands came up to me just as Ned Sherrin was beginning the audience 'warm-up' before the start of the show, and he said, 'We've made some tea in the scene dock – would you like to come in there and have some with us?'

Actually, I wanted to listen to the warm-up, because

I'd heard it was more risqué than the show. But he said, 'That's not the sort of thing for young girls like you, dear. You're better off having a nice cup of tea than hearing all those rude jokes.'

I was about twenty-nine then, certainly twenty-eight.

BEN PALMER *Engineer*

The early Lime Grove cameras tended to have a flicker, which could be improved by de-focusing electronically.

One day a phone call from a viewer was put right through to me in the control gallery. He said he had just built his own set – a lot of people did that in those days – but it had a strange flicker; could I give him any advice?

I said, 'Well, watch it now,' and I turned the defocusing slightly.

'That's better,' said the viewer and rang off.

DAVID WILSON *Managing Director, Southern TV*

When Southern Television had just been established, there was some difference of opinion between them and Associated-Rediffusion over payment for programmes. At the time, Rediffusion had got into the habit of inviting all the companies in turn to lunch and, in spite of the row going on, it came round to Southern's turn. When Rediffusion asked how many of our board would be turning up, they were rather horrified to find the number of members we'd be bringing, because it meant they'd have to elongate their reproduction Regency dining-room table. However, they got their scenery department to make an extra leaf to go in and managed to accommodate us all.

The table was superbly laid when we arrived, with beautiful candelabra and heavy glasses, heavy everything, but the lunch was not a happy occasion – lots of acrimony developing and sparks flying. Over coffee, our Graham Dowson and a member of the Rediffusion board were having one hell of an argument on their own. Both of them were big heavy men and they were sitting opposite each other, leaning hard on the table. By chance it happened to be at the place where the new leaf had been inserted and suddenly there was a tremendous crash. The new leaf split right the way across and a large candelabra went through the gaping hole onto the floor. Whereupon, the rest of the table-cloth from both sides was pulled in by the weight, and everybody's glasses, coffee-cups and plates disappeared down it, leaving an empty table.

There was a stunned silence. Then, purple with rage, their Chairman, John Spencer Wills, looked across at our Chairman, John Davis, and said, 'You not only won't pay for our programmes, but you come here and smash up our furniture!'

At which, I leapt to my feet in defence and said, 'This example of Rediffusion workmanship is why we won't pay for your programmes.'

ROGER APPLETON *Vision Control Engineer*
When I started in ITV we did four live shows a week at the Chelsea Palace, including *The Army Game*. The boys in that – Alfie Bass, Harry Fowler, Bernard Bresslaw, all of them – they were always playing practical jokes on each other. There was one show where Harry had to come off-stage, have a haversack put on his back and get back immediately to assemble on-stage with the rest of the soldiers. Well, the lads loaded a stage-weight into the haversack. Harry had no option but to go on with 25 lb of stage-weight on his back.

PAUL FOX *Editor*
Those were the days when some of the *Sportsview* team used to get to football matches in a specially chartered helicopter with a big *BBC Sportsview* label plastered all over it.

And one Sunday afternoon I was at home when the phone rang and it was none other than the Director General himself, Sir Ian Jacob – and he said, 'What on earth is your helicopter doing hovering over Princess Margaret's home?'

I said, 'I've got no idea – our charter ends on Saturday night.'

Well, it took me quite a while to unravel the story, but

The *Sportsview* helicopter

it was the time of the Princess Margaret/Group Captain Townsend romance and I eventually discovered that because they were guests for the weekend with friends down at Uckfield, the *Daily Mirror* had chartered the helicopter for surveillance purposes.

What they'd neglected to do, however, was take the *Sportsview* tags off it. So when Margaret and Townsend saw this thing hovering above them, they not unnaturally wanted to kick hell out of the BBC.

MIKE SCOTT *Director*

There was one character in *Coronation Street* we had great difficulty in casting. We could not find an Ena Sharples. Tony Warren had written her as a very awkward dictatorial lady, but of course it was also essential that she had to be liked, indeed loved. Try as we might we could not find an actress who could give us those two qualities.

We got desperate, and we had a meeting of Harry Latham, Derek Bennett, the other director, myself and, I think, Cecil Bernstein, because he was the grandfather of *Coronation Street*, and Harry Elton. We agreed to have one last go to find an Ena. If we couldn't, the character would be written out.

Vi Carson with (*left*) Lynne Carol, (*right*) Margot Bryant and Arthur Leslie

There were six more actresses to audition. We went to unusual lengths to get the auditions right. They were rehearsed for a day and then put on closed circuit. Derek had three to audition and I had the other three and then we both looked at the results on the closed-circuit screen. We'd done the scene in the first episode of *Coronation Street* where Ena makes her entrance into the corner shop. We were both despondent about all our ladies. Then Vi Carson came on the screen and was wonderful. She got the job, of course, and I said to Derek, because Vi was one of his three, 'Why were you so despondent?'

He said, 'Because she didn't do that when I rehearsed her.'

So we talked to her and Vi said, 'Well, I didn't like what we'd done at rehearsals, to be honest. So I thought – because I don't really need this job you know, I don't think I'm going to stay longer than six weeks – I thought I'd do it my way!'

DIANA PARRY *Producer's Assistant*
In the early ITV days, we did some programmes at the Wood Green Empire with the Crazy Gang. The last sketch in one of the shows was supposed to end with the Gang pulling something which made the whole set fall down. But when we came to the transmission, they pulled it too early. and the set came down halfway through the sketch.

And because the director had nothing else we could go to once our set had collapsed, all he could do was put up the closing credit-titles. Consequently, the programme finished several minutes early.

Afterwards, Jack Hylton's production manager came into the control gallery and reduced me to tears by implying it was all my fault because I was the one responsible for the timing of the show. Then, later, when we were having a drink with all the cast, the Gang confessed they had deliberately pulled the set down early because they were cross about something.

RICHARD LEVIN *Head of Design*
George Djurkovic was one of the new breed of set designers, an architect. He came to me one day and said, 'This man Bill Cotton, this terrible producer fellow, what does he think I am? You know what he wants me to design? A red-nosed reindeer! Me – an ARIBA!'

So I rang Bill. 'What's this I hear from George about you wanting him to design a reindeer with a red nose? That's a bit off, isn't it?'

And he said, 'Not really. There's a new song out that is actually called "Rudolf, The Red Nosed Reindeer".'

BINNIE MARCUS *Production Assistant*
We were recording a concert at the Albert Hall with Leopold Stokowski. I believe it was his eightieth birthday. We got the OK from TV Centre that they were recording, so we cued Stokowski to enter.

He received a thunderous reception, a standing ovation. It was really tremendous – very emotional. He bowed and took his place and I should think it took a whole minute for the audience to settle down again.

The music started and it had been going on for perhaps another minute, when TV Centre rang through. 'Look, sorry, but a bit of a mess-up here. Could you start again, please.'

Antony Craxton, the producer, found this so unbelievable, for a while he couldn't speak for laughing. Then, still having difficulty getting the words out, he said to the Stage Manager, 'Just get Stokowski to go out and come in again, would you?'

YVONNE LLOYD *Production Assistant*
There's an apocryphal Southern TV story, though Trevor the Weather always denies it ... It could have been Julian (Pettifer).

The story was that, on one live transmission, he didn't realise until the little weather-board appeared on the screen that in the word 'fog' which was showing over our area, the letter 'f' had dropped off.

So he came back and said, 'I'm terribly sorry, I must apologise for the 'f' in fog.'

JOHN LANE *Floor Manager*
Somebody up in front of a board for the Floor Manager's job is reputed to have been asked, 'What would you do if you had an elephant in your studio and it went berserk and stamped on the floor and fell through it?'

The prospective Floor Manager said, 'Well, if the elephant fell through the floor, it wouldn't be in my studio, would it?'

BILL COTTON *Assistant Head of Light Entertainment*
When Tom Sloan was Head of Light Entertainment he
was over at the Albert Hall one year organising the
Eurovision Song Contest. He was an exceedingly able
organiser, so while I was having lunch with Terry
Henebery, Roger Ordish, Bryan Whitehouse and a
couple of other young producers, I said, 'It's all going
far too well. Why don't we cause a little alarm down
there?'

We came up with the idea of sending an Albanian
delegation along, wanting to join the Contest. As we
talked about it, it got funnier and funnier and I said,
'Well, maybe this evening.'

So about half-past four they turned up at my office.
All of them had been to Wardrobe Department and got
themselves decked-out in these European-looking costumes. I said, 'Well, let's just be a bit careful, we don't
want to foul things up if there are any real problems. Let
me go on ahead and I'll give you the nod if it's all OK.'

But when I got to the Albert Hall, sure enough it was
all going like clockwork and there was Tom sitting behind this enormous desk having a quiet after-rehearsal
drink with Jim Moir, who was running the studio floor,
and John Stringer who was looking after administration.
So I made the phone call to set the thing going, then I
said to Tom, 'Have you heard anything from the
Albanian delegation?'

Tom said, 'What Albanian delegation?'

'Well, they pitched up at TV Centre and I told them
to come along here.'

'No, I haven't heard anything.'

I looked out of the window and there below was this
enormous car. I said, 'Well, they've obviously got some
money, they're just getting out of a Rolls Bentley.'

They were all looking around out there and acting up
marvellously. Tom said, 'What are they doing here? I
can't understand it.'

That was the moment when it was all hanging in the
balance and he could say, 'Ridiculous, someone must be
having a practical joke,' which was why, when John

Stringer said, 'I'd better go down and see them,' I said to him quietly, 'Let them come up here.'

Roger Ordish could speak a bit of Russian and they'd brought a girl with them – I think she worked for the *Daily Sketch* – who was pretty European-looking, and she acted as interpreter, saying they wanted to sing in the Eurovision Song Contest.

Tom started off quite politely, saying that was out of the question, because Albania wasn't even part of Eurovision. But she wasn't having any of that. She pleaded: 'You must understand – if you turn us away we could not go back to our country. We would be disgraced ... You are a big man ... You could permit us to sing. We have a wonderful song.'

Tom began getting agitated. 'No, you have to understand I haven't got the authority.'

Eventually he said, 'Ask them if they'd like a drink.' She asked them, they said something back in gobbledygook, so now here was Tom pouring out drinks for his own young producers.

Then the interpreter said, 'You must let them sing their song.' Our own British entry that year was 'Congratulations', sung by Cliff Richard. What they then proceeded to sing was a gobbledy-gook version of that.

Actually, it was Queenie, Tom's secretary, who suddenly said, 'Hey, that's Terry Henebery.' Tom not only took the whole thing in good part, he made us repeat it all again when my mother came along to meet me there that evening.

MICHAEL MILLS *Producer*

I still remember the first show I ever produced, the Harry Parry sextet on 20 January 1947, and that awful first moment when I had to say, 'Fade up, Camera One' – never before having given an order anywhere and knowing that the moment I delivered that one the nation's next half-hour of television would be entirely in my hands.

But as there were only about 50,000 sets altogether at that time of which perhaps 5,000 would be switched on during a Wednesday afternoon, and out of those there probably wouldn't be more than 2,000 people actually watching, it really didn't matter much if I made a few mistakes.

As it happens, apart from two occasions when I had Harry Parry speaking to the wrong camera it came out all right – and from that moment on, I was a fully-fledged producer.

FRANK HOLLAND *Property Assistant*
I'll always remember the day – it was in 1949, I believe – when we first got pictures out of the studio as far as Birmingham. I rushed up to Alexandra Palace just to be able to say I was in the studio on that day. We could not believe that a hundred miles away they were seeing our picture.

Glossary

AP, Ally Pally	Alexandra Palace, first home of British television.
AR	Associated-Rediffusion.
BH	Broadcasting House.
Dry	to forget lines/words.
Corpse	to collapse in laughter.
Dolly	a movable camera mount.
LE	Light Entertainment.
Lighting gantry	platform or scaffolding high up in a studio from which studio lights are positioned.
Lime Grove	Lime Grove studios, Shepherd's Bush.
Mix	to fade one camera to another electronically between camera shots.
OB	Outside Broadcast.
PA	we have used this throughout in its ITV sense, i.e. Production Assistant
Pan	to move camera horizontally left to right or up or down or vice versa.
Peel	picture explodes, or disintegrates to white.
Perspective steps	steps painted and built to give an illusion of steps. Non practical.
Rig	to take vision and sound equipment from an OB van and set it up at a location. But a de-rig takes control equipment from the OB van to set up a temporary control point in a building; as at Westminster Abbey.
Roving Eye Camera	a camera mounted on the roof of a specially equipped Outside Broadcast van.
Scene dock	a place where scenery is stored.
Telecine	machine used for transmitting film on television.
Tracker	a member of camera crew who pushes the dolly.
Turret mountings	mounts to hold a number of selected lenses.
Voice-over	commentary over picture.
Zoom lens	a camera lens with variable focal length.

The Contributors

Cliff Adams. Studied piano and organ. Became dance-band pianist. After RAF service was arranger for many leading bands. Formed top fifties vocal group, The Stargazers, and the Adam Singers for BBC Show Band. Songwriter and composer of many TV commercials.

Roger Adams. An accountant who joined Anglo-Scottish, working with David Paul Tingay, former ballet dancer, to make commercials. They did the first TV commercial. Was writer and producer of the famous Schweppes 'You Know Who' series with William Franklyn. Now freelance producer working in advertising and documentaries.

Elizabeth Agombar. Joined BBC TV Wardrobe, as it then was, in the 1950s from the theatre. Became costume designer for many drama productions including *Spread of the Eagle* and the Roman plays of Shakespeare, and for major opera and music programmes. Retired in 1970 to take up another of her great interests – antiques.

Roger Appleton. After training at Oxford College of Technology, was an engineer at the Atomic Energy Research Establishment, Harwell. Joined BBC TV engineering, then was a vision control engineer at Granada. Joined AR. Later Director of Engineering LWT. Fellow RTS.

Nick Barker. A BBC reporter, he joined AR as assistant editor, *This Week*; later editor and presenter of the TV cinema programme, *Close-up*. Was also an ITN reporter. Returned to BBC TV and was one of the presenters of the BBC2 *News*. Spent ten years working in Spain. Channel 4 *Years Ahead* programme presenter.

Charles Beard. Started with Middlesex Fire Brigade; then became fireman at Wood Green Empire and was taken over by ATV as 'part of the inventory' when the Empire became TV studio. Was ATV's first employee. Remained as security officer until he retired in 1975.

Michael Bond. Creator of Paddington Bear. BBC radio engineer 1942. After the forces, returned to Monitoring Service BBC in 1947. Transferred to TV where he was senior cameraman until 1965. He resigned to work full-time on Paddington books and to start his own film company. Also writes novels.

Peter Bostock. Joined J. Walter Thompson, London, as copywriter, progressing to Deputy Group Creative Director. Was supervisor of Benson and Bowles. Rejoined JWT becoming Head of Creative Department. Now Creative Director for Charles Barker City.

Sally Ann Bragg. Was trained at London College of Fashion; did a comprehensive course in the art and craft of beauty, hairdressing and wig-making. In BBC television became a make-up supervisor and was one of the first to do make-up for colour TV. Is now freelance make-up artist.

Ricky Briggs. Started his career in documentary films. Joined BBC 1953 as assistant cameraman in Sequence Section. Joined Film Department as cameraman at AR 1955. Returned to work in film industry in 1968 and is now a director of photography in films and TV commercials.

Stephen Bundy. Joined TV Scenic Design at Alexandra Palace pre-war. Designed all the early Dickens series. There were 3 designers when he joined TV; he ended his career in charge of 150 design staff. Retired; still lectures on design.

Sir Alastair Burnet. Started his career as a journalist on the *Glasgow Herald* then became leader writer on *The Economist*; political editor ITN; editor of *The Economist*; editor *Daily Express*. First newscaster on ITN's *News at Ten* with Andrew Gardner. Won Richard Dimbleby Award at BAFTA 1966, 1970 and 1979. Now Director and Newscaster ITN. Knighted New Year 1984.

Derek Burrell-Davis. Finished wartime service as Lt Colonel in Sudan Defence Force. Joined Rank Organisation to learn about film. Joined BBC in London 1950. Started TV in the north. Returned to London TV OBs as a producer in 1955. Specialised in circus spectaculars. Then Head of Network Production Centre, Manchester, with a staff of 700. Retired after twenty-six years in broadcasting.

Hal Burton. Trained in acting; also qualified as an architect. Joined BBC TV and became, unusually, a drama producer who did his own set designs. Outstanding productions include *The Man Shakespeare*; *An Elizabethan Evening* and *Great Actors*. Now retired and writing a book on church architecture.

George Campey OBE. Former *Evening Standard* television correspondent, who moved to BBC TV from Fleet Street to succeed Huw Wheldon as Television Publicity Officer. Three years later became Head of BBC Publicity Department, until retirement in 1976. Served three BBC Director Generals: Sir Ian Jacob, Sir Hugh Greene and Sir Charles Curran.

Sybil Cave. Joined TV at Alexandra Palace in 1946 as production secretary to Fred O'Donovan; worked on the plays of Shaw, Sean O' Casey, Priestley and Yeats. Later worked in Bristol with producer Brandon Acton-Bond. After a short time as a freelance PA returned to BBC London and joined Artists Contracts where she is now Senior Contracts Assistant.

Richard Cawston. Joined BBC TV in 1947 as a film editor. From 1950–4 produced the original TV newsreel for nearly 700 editions. Moved to studio production as co-editor *Panorama*. Since 1955 has written, directed and produced documentary films; was first Head of Documentary Programmes in 1965. Won many awards including the Prix Italia and Desmond Davis Award. Currently Executive Video Arts Television.

James Cellan Jones. Joined BBC TV in 1955. Graduated from AFM to producer. After twelve years became a freelance director, in films and theatre as well as TV. Rejoined BBC TV in 1976 as Head of Plays. Award winners include *The Scarlet and the Black*; *The Forsyte Sage*; *Roads to Freedom*. Now works freelance. Directed LWT series *A Fine Romance* and BBC *Oxbridge Blues* play series.

Colin Clewes. Was BBC OB sound engineer in Manchester in 1941. After Royal Navy, rejoined as one of the first camera trackers post-war. Cameraman 1948; productions ranged from *Rooftop Rendezvous* to *Oedipus Rex*. Went to ATV at the start in charge of cameras; became a director six months later. Specialised in quiz games and LE. Won awards for *Morecambe and Wise*, and the Marty Feldman series. Currently with Central TV.

Barney Colehan. Served with British Forces Network. Post-war, produced radio's *Have a Go* (became known from Wilfred Pickle's phrase, 'Give 'em the money, Barney'). Seven years later moved to television. Was producer *Good Old Days* for thirty years. Retired after thirty-seven years in the same BBC Leeds office. Now freelance.

Bill Cotton OBE. Joined BBC TV in 1956 as a contract LE producer, moving from his music business with Johnny 'Jingles' Johnston. Produced series like *Show Band Show*, *Off the Record*, *Juke Box Jury* and *Six Five Special*; his main work was producing his father's series *The Billy Cotton Band Show*. From 1962 to 1977 held top LE posts and developed such shows as *Morecambe and Wise*; *The Frost Report*; *The Two Ronnies*. became Controller BBC 1. Later Managing Director, BBC TV 1984. Fellow RTS.

Mary Crewe. Went to Rediffusion as an agency secretarial 'temp' for a week. Is still in television after twenty-seven years. Became a PA in Schools Programmes and is now a PA with Thames TV.

Charles de Jaeger. Came to BBC in 1943 from journalism and war service with the Free French film unit. Joined BBC European Service and moved as a sound film cameraman to TV *Newsreel*. Directed and shot *Round the World in Eight Days*. Became studio lighting cameraman in 1955 directing film stories for *Panorama*, *Tonight* and *Monitor* and drama sequences. Now freelance.

Peter Dimmock OBE. Ex-RAF pilot. Was post-war reporter with Press Association. Joined OBs at AP at restart of TV as producer/ commentator. Presented weekly *Sportsview*. Was General Manager of TV OBs from 1954–72. Became Chief Executive of Television Enterprises. On leaving BBC joined American Broadcasting Companies Inc in New York 1977. Is currently Vice-President and MD of ABC Sport International. Fellow RTS.

Tiny Durham. Was a BBC radio engineer in 1936. While still working as a senior radio OB engineer in Glasgow he transferred to television in 1952 when TV came to Scotland. Moved down from Scotland to Wembley OB Planning Office, becoming a senior planning and lighting engineer. Is now retired.

Keith Edelsten. Joined BBC TV from sound OBs 1938 as an engineer. After RAF returned as an engineer in London control room, moved to TV in 1949. Was one of first engineers to 'open up' Lime Grove; became a Technical Operations Manager. Worked on LE shows including the innovative *Hit Parade*; on *The Onedin Line*, *Z-cars*, and *Animal, Vegetable, Mineral?* Saw colour TV in and retired in 1972.

Polly Elwes. Came into television because her birthday was 29 February. She wrote to Cecil Madden suggesting a programme for people who had a birthday only every four years. After the programme she presented afternoon programmes and became an announcer. She was the first woman TV reporter on *Tonight*. Later freelanced.

Jim Entwhistle. Was a reporter, then sub-editor for a number of Northern papers; joined BBC's Northern newsroom as an assistant news editor, from the Manchester Evening News in 1954. Became Editor, *Look North* in 1961, and later Information Officer, then Press and Promotions Officer for 18 years until his retirement.

Cynthia Felgate. Joined BBC TV in 1963 as an AFM from a drama-teaching and acting background. Became Production Assistant with the production team which started *Play School*, and two years later became its producer. Since 1969 has been Executive Producer for all BBC TV programmes for younger children.

Sir Denis Forman. Ended his army career as Lt Colonel and joined Central Office of Information Films Division. Became Director of British Film Institute. Joined Granada Television in 1955 and was first producer of *What the Papers Say*. After ten years making programmes became Chairman of Granada TV in 1974. Instigated the television drama series *The Jewel in the Crown*. Was knighted in 1976. Is still Granada Television's very active Chairman.

Patricia ('Paddy') Foy. Studied at Royal Academy of Music. Was ASM to English National Opera. Joined BBC TV as a music producer in the early fifties. Produced *Music For You*, *Gala Performance*, many ballets and music profiles. Her recent award winners were *Magic of Dance* with Margot Fonteyn and *Profile in Music* with Beverly Sills. Now freelance and is co-directing with Rudolf Nureyev *Romeo and Juliet*. Is fellow of Royal Academy of Music.

Gwen Foyle. Joined TV early fifties as production secretary from radio. Worked at Lime Grove with producers Norman Swallow and Stephen Hearst in documentaries. On Coronation OB with Peter Dimmock. Was Producer's Assistant in Drama in 1957, working on plays, operas, serials and series.

Paul Fox OBE. After war service Parachute Regiment, journalistic experience with *Kentish Times*, and *Pathe News*, became script-writer for the pioneer TV *Newsreel*. 1953 devised *Sportsview*; edited it for six years. Was editor of *Panorama* and later Head of Current Affairs Group. Was Controller BBC 1 for six years, then Yorkshire TV's Director of Programmes, and since 1976 Managing Director of Yorkshire TV.

Roland Fox MBE. Was a journalist in his native Derby before six years of the army, during which became Military Assistant to Montgomery's Chief of Staff. Resumed career in Fleet Street. Joined BBC, where, as Parliamentary Correspondent in the fifties, he made regular 'live' broadcasts. Was first broadcasting journalist elected Chairman of Parliamentary Press Gallery. Became Chief Assistant to Editor of News and Current Affairs.

Don Gale. After British Forces Network joined BBC as sound engineer; became TV studio cameraman at Lime Grove. Joined AR 1955. Set up first TV station in Africa (Nigeria); also Liberian Broadcasting Service. Director Producer at Rediffusion and LWT; and Managing Director Rediffusion TV in Hong Kong for seven years. Had own consultancy, then with Columbia TV. Now Vice-President MCA TV London.

Andrew Gardner. Started broadcasting career in Rhodesia. Returned to Britain and joined BBC World Service as a reporter. Joined ITN when it started in 1961 and was in the driving seat of the first *News at Ten*. Was ITV commentator for Princess Anne's wedding. After fifteen years at ITN joined Thames where he presents Thames *News*.

Vic Gardiner OBE. Started as sound radio engineer, then went to TV at Lime Grove to train as cameraman. Joined AR as senior cameraman. *Little Gertie, the Lamplighter's Darling* was his first programme from Granville Theatre at start of ITV. Became Head of Studio Production, Rediffusion. Joined LWT as Productions Controller. Later Director and General Manager, LWT.

Norma Gilbert. Joined newly formed BBC TV publicity unit of four at Alexandra Palace in 1951. As television grew and developed so did the unit. Became TV Press Officer for twelve years until 1974. Also had programme attachments to *Blue Peter* and radio's Archive Features. Now freelances as arts and entertainments publicist.

Rosemary Gill. Joined BBC TV from radio 1951 as guest producer's secretary. Became AFM in the fifties; worked on music and ballet, schools and children's drama and with *Blue Peter*, becoming first producer and later assistant editor. Suggested idea of *Multi-Coloured Swap Shop*, and became its editor. In 1983 set up own video production company, Keepsakes Video.

John P. Hamilton. Was pre-war sound radio engineer. After RAF, returned to mobile sound recording. Joined AR as sound engineer; later became vision-mixer and then a director. Directed the popular *Stars and Garters* series. Moved to OBs. In 1968 joined LWT. Retired but looks after LWT archives.

Derek Harper. Was sound engineer with Marconi OB Unit and sound balanced the first 200 *Tonight* programmes. Joined AR where he was videotape engineer and Operations Supervisor. Joined LWT where he became Senior Supervisory Engineer, Videotape Recording.

Sybil Harper (formerly Wynne). Trained as a technical assistant in radio. Later became a producer's assistant in television OBs. Resigned to be a freelance researcher. First event was Churchill State Funeral finding material for twenty-six foreign commentators. Specialised in State and Royal events first for BBC and for last 12 years for ITV. Has had over 100 articles published. Was joint contributor on *Miles of London* book.

Bimbi Harris. Was radio recording engineer. Went to AP at restart of television as a vision-mixer; this included a variety of jobs including that of cameraman, thus she was the first woman to operate a television camera, in the fifties. Later she joined A-R; became a director. With re-allocation of licenses became a director with LWT from which she retired recently.

Stephen Hearst CBE. Joined television at AP in 1952 as a relief script-writer, becoming a script-writer director. Produced *The Glory That Was Greece* with Sir Compton McKenzie, and *The Grandeur That Was Rome* with Sir Mortimer Wheeler. Became Executive Producer Arts Programmes then Head of Arts Features. Moved to radio as Controller Radio 3. Special Adviser to BBC's DG.

Douglas Hespe. Worked in sound radio on *ITMA* from 1945–6. After national service returned to BBC and joined OBs as an SM. Became a producer/director. Now regularly directs *My Music*, among numerous other OBs.

Trevor Hill. Was a junior programme engineer in radio. Moved to television; became a director and producer of children's TV in Manchester. Returned to radio and became Network Editor, Radio, North Region. Is writing a book on his years in broadcasting called *Life with my Favourite Aunt*.

Christine Hillcoat. Came to BBC Engineering Division in 1942 during the war, having trained and worked previously in hairdressing and beauty culture. Transferred to Make-up in 1964. Made up artists in such trail-blazing productions as *Quatermass*, *1984*, *Maigret* and *Dr Finlay's Casebook*. Was Head of Make-up until her retirement in 1973.

W. 'Bill' Hillman. Came from the film industry to Buying Department at BH. Joined AP 1938 in Scenic Services; became a TV props buyer. When told that TV did a whole show for £50, Bill said, 'You don't want a buyer, you want a cadger'; so until 1939 says he learned to cadge rather than buy. Post-war, returned to TV as props buyer and helped build a property store of thousands of items. Was an Assistant Property Master until he retired in 1968.

Frank Holland. Started as a page boy 1938 at BH and AP. Then was a clerk to BBC Evesham until conscripted. Rejoined TV on demob in 1947, as a clerk for BBC TV's first Head of Design. He catalogued all furniture, scenery, props, on a system still used. Later became Assistant Property Master, Property Organiser and then Manager. Prop items numbered in tens when he started and in thousands when he retired in 1983.

H.W. 'Jacko' Jackson. Was recording engineer BBC radio 1940. Moved to television as a film sound recordist going on royal tours and various assignments at home and abroad. Became Film Planning Manager. Is now retired.

Johnny Johnston. Known as the Jingles King – not surprisingly, as he was one of the original jingles writers of TV commercials, he has written words and music for over 3,000 jingles, also signature tunes for radio, including *Take It From Here*. Started his career in publishing with Bill Cotton. He had a band called the Johnston Brothers which topped the charts in its day. He still composes jingles.

Mary Keene. Was a London fire officer during the war. Then one of the first women account executives working on conference design until 1950. Joined TV as secretary to Peter Dimmock. Then became PA and worked on early OBs including *The Goodwin Lightship*. Moved to Current Affairs, where she became a production assistant and later specialised on party conferences. Retired in 1979.

Joan Kemp-Welch. A theatre director in London's West End, she went to television for the start of A-R. Was one of the first woman directors in TV. She stayed with A-R throughout their existence; she won five major TV awards and was the first woman to be given the Desmond Davis Award. Since 1967 she has freelanced, working for BBC and other major independent companies. She continues to direct stage plays here and abroad, her career spanning thirty years.

Jack Kine. Joined BBC TV as a scenic artist in 1938. Rejoined after war service and together with Bernard Wilkie was co-founder of the innovative Visual Effects set-up in BBC TV Design, formed around the time *1984* was produced. The *Quatermass* series, *Dr Who and the Daleks* and *It's a Square World* contained his meticulous, weird, and wonderful model-making. Is author of books on scenic model-making and kites.

John Lane. Came to television in 1963 as a Floor Manager, from Wyndham theatres where he was assistant to the General Manager. Worked in various programme areas including *Tonight* and on the original *Jackanory*. Became producer on *Play School*.

Verity Lambert. Was an ABC TV PA in 1961 with *Armchair Theatre*. Joined Sydney Newman at BBC to produce *Dr Who*. Moved to LWT to produce *Budgie* and *Between the Wars*. Returned to BBC TV to produce *Shoulder to Shoulder*. Joined Thames TV as Controller, Drama Department. Developed many acclaimed series and plays including *Rock Follies*, *Edward and Mrs Simpson*, and the award-winning *The Naked Civil Servant*. Became an executive for Euston films, and then Production Director, Thorne EMI Screen Entertainment.

Michael Latham. Was a newspaper reporter in Bristol. Joined BBC TV as trainee director in television OBs in 1959. Specialised in science programmes in the then new Features and Science Department. Worked on *Horizon*, edited *Tomorrow's World* and *Man Alive*. Won British Academy award for *Explorers* series. Left BBC to work as independent producer. Most recent work with Video Arts Television.

Richard Levin OBE. In 1951 designed the Festival of Britain Travelling Exhibition. Joined BBC TV as Head of Design in 1953. Designed sets, from *Joan Gilbert's Diary* to the *Eurovision Song Contest*. Became Head of Design Group in 1967, formed for colour TV co-ordinating scenic design, costume, make-up and graphics. Launched BBC Enterprises Exhibitions with costumes and sets from *The Six Wives of Henry VIII* at the V & A Museum, which later went on tour. Author of *Television by Design*.

Yvonne Littlewood. Started as a secretary in radio; after two years transferred to TV becoming a producer's secretary, then PA. Became producer/director for BBC TV LE, their only woman producer for many years. Since then has about 500 programmes under her belt, featuring Val Doonican, Nana Mouskouri, Petula Clark, Keith Michell, and Count Basie, and specials with Andrew Lloyd Webber, Nat King Cole, Perry Como, Duke Ellington and James Galway. Has won three special awards.

Innes Lloyd. Trained as an actor at Central School of Speech and Drama. Served in Royal Navy. Joined BBC World Service as studio manager. Moved to TV Presentation 1954. Was television OBs producer for six years, then Drama. Productions include *Dr Who*, and such epics as *Life After Death* and *An Englishman Abroad*. BAFTA award in 1981 for *Going Gently*.

Yvonne Lloyd. Joined Southern TV at its start in 1958 on programme publicity. Moved to the regional magazine programme *Day by Day* when it began as PA for editor John Boorman. Is now features producer for *Coast to Coast* with TVS.

Babette Loraine. Was a trained beautician, and after Ambulance Service in the war, joined BBC TV as a make-up assistant, remaining with them until 1955. Became Head of Make-up for ATV until 1961.

Cecil Madden. Was first producer in TV and creator of the weekly *Picture Page*. Previously started Empire Service 1933. During war, was Head of Programmes for all the forces. Returned to TV as Programme Planner, when his budget for a week's programmes was £1,000. Produced first programme to re-open the service. Started Children's TV programmes, then was in charge of special projects up to and after the start of BBC 2. Author and translator of plays.

Violet Maitland ('Matey'). Worked as a dresser pre-war in London theatres. Joined BBC TV in 1938 as one of the first two television dressers ever. Rejoined when television restarted at AP and then was at Lime Grove and worked to retirement. When interviewed had just reached eighty but looked maybe fifty-five. Now lives in Scotland.

Binnie Marcus (née Goldberg). Began as secretary with BBC Engineering. Transferred to television and worked on *This is Your Life* and *Sportsview*. Became PA to Anthony Craxton in TV OBs working on many royal events. Resigned in the early sixties when she married.

Joan Marsden MBE. Served in WAAF and after demob was Stage Manager in London's West End theatres before joining BBC TV in 1957 as an AFM, becoming FM in 1961. Known as 'Mum' to everyone including prime ministers. She was warded the MBE in 1978; is now retired.

Stewart Marshall. Joined BBC TV in 1952 as holiday relief draughtsman. Became a design assistant and in 1955 a designer. Was colour expert in Design Department, working with the experimental colour unit at AP. Up to 1966 designed around 600 studio sets including all general election programmes until 1970; science spectaculars such as *The Violent Universe* and *Telstar* and *Earlybird* programme sets.

Mike Metcalfe. Worked for British Relay Wireless then joined A-R. Was Supervisory Engineer of a Remotes Unit (as OBs were called for a short time). Became Programme Liaison Engineer at Rediffusion 1962. Is now producer, writer and director for the National Maritime Institute film unit.

Leonard Miall OBE. Joined BBC External Services as German Talks Editor 1939. Post-war BBC Washington Correspondent. In 1954 became head of TV Talks. Spent two years in the sixties planning BBC2, before returning to America as US Representative. In 1971 became Controller International Relations. Since 1975 has been BBC's research historian. His contribution is from his Radio 3 *In At The Start*.

Vicki Miller. Worked at Ealing Film Studios on such films as *The Lavender Hill Mob*. Joined A-R at the start of ITV as a PA and continued this until her retirement last year.

Andrew Miller-Jones. Worked in film studios in the early talkies. Joined television at AP in 1937. Pioneer of TV talks and specialised in early science programmes, such as photographing the moon through specially constructed telescope in 1947. Took charge of television production training. Held an executive television post at EEC in Brussels. Is now retired.

Michael Mills. Was a sound drama effects boy before the war. After Navy service worked in the theatre, then joined BBC TV as first specialist LE producer. Originated and produced *The Passing Shows* and the first situation comedy series *Family Affairs*; later series such as *The World of Wooster*, *Blandings Castle* and *Misleading Cases*. Head of BBC TV Comedy in 1967. Returned to producing and directing in 1971. Now a freelance producer and director.

Alasdair Milne. Joined BBC 1954 radio production; came to TV as producer. Became Deputy Editor *Tonight*, later Editor. Left BBC to freelance. Rejoined, becoming Controller, Scotland. Succeeded David Attenborough as Director of Programmes. In 1982 became Director General of the BBC.

Royston Morley. Transferred from radio to TV in 1937 and worked on *Picture Page*. Post-war was drama producer responsible for many trail-blazing productions including Priestley's *Dangerous Corner*; a 1947 rendering of *Mourning Becomes Electra* and the Festival of Britain play, *The Final Test* by Terence Rattigan. Left BBC TV in 1957 to help start Australian TV. Returned to Britain joining ATV. Still works as freelance producer.

Peter Morley OBE. Wrote and directed documentary films before joining A-R at the start. Among his award-winning programmes was the *Life and Times of Lord Mountbatten*. Since working freelance has made programmes for BBC and Yorkshire TV. Now Controller of Programmes Thorn-EMI Video. Fellow RTS.

Alan Mouncer. Joined BBC 1946 as junior engineer in Redruth Cornwall. After RAF returned in 1951 as an engineer then moved to TV as a cameraman. From 1960 was OB Stage Manager; became OB Director.

Sydney Newman. Brought from Canada to Head ABC Drama. Was responsible for *Armchair Theatre* and devised *The Avengers*. Moved to BBC TV as Head of Drama Group. Was responsible for *The Wednesday Play*, *The Forsyte Saga*, *Hamlet at Elsinore* and *Dr Who*, among innovative drama, and operas such as *Billy Budd*. Returned to Canada in 1970. Now in England to produce for Channel Four.

Ronnie Noble. Started with *Children's Newsreel*. Covered the Korean war as a film cameraman. Returned to work on TV *Newsreel*. Then worked on numerous sporting epics such as live coverage of Winter Olympics in 1956. Became Editor *Grandstand*. Retired from BBC. Now TV consultant.

Lord Orr-Ewing. Was an Outside Broadcast assistant to Philip Dorté in pre-war TV at AP. After service in the RAF returned to BBC for re-start of TV. Resigned to become MP for Hendon North.

Ben Palmer. Joined BBC sound engineering 1947 transferred to TV in 1949 and was one of first six engineers at Lime Grove studios. Has name on patent for first television prompter. Fellow RTS.

Bill Parkinson. Joined TV as Floor Manager after being a Stage Manager provincial repertory. As FM worked on programmes from LE to Current Affairs. Succeeded Joan Marsden on *Panorama*. Is now Head of Scenic Operations.

Diana Parry. Was production secretary with Tom Arnold, working with Noël Coward and Robert Nesbitt. Worked on Marshall Plan in Paris. Became a casting director with Rediffusion in 1963. Is now Head of Casting at LWT.

Sylvia Peters. Started in the theatre in musicals such as *The Night and the Music*. Gained a teaching qualification in dancing. Was one of first post-war women TV announcers. Presented OBs such as *Come Dancing*. Later worked for Southern TV especially on admags.

George Pettican. Joined TV's Lime Grove studios from Riverside Film Studios as one of television's first prop men, when 'we not only looked after props but did scene-setting too'. Became known as 'one of the best property buyers in the business'. Retired in 1973.

Bill Podmore. Was a pilot in the RAF, then joined Marconi Marine. Joined BBC as a trainee cameraman. At start of ITV joined ATV and then Granada TV where he has produced *Coronation Street* for last nine years.

Ros Pool. Joined TV at AP in 1947 working on all kinds of programmes. Was production secretary to Drama producers and worked on first Dickens serial in early fifties. Later on early *Z-Cars* and *Maigret*. Job developed into that of a production assistant in Plays department. She retired 1984.

Jim Pople. Was assistant film editor at Denham, Pinewood and Army Film Unit. Joined BBC Film department. Later joined A-R as a film editor/director. Transferred to live TV in 1957 directing in Children's Documentaries and Features until he joined OBs. Continued in OBs with Thames TV. Now specialises in royal events and has directed twenty royal film premières.

Pamela Pyer. Joined BBC TV Press Office from Radio in 1960 as photo clerk until 1973, when she resigned to do teacher training, and after qualifying taught at ILEA schools. Now works for the British Astronomical Association and is a qualified City of London guide.

Alan Protheroe. After three years on the *Glamorgan Gazette* and National Service joined BBC Wales and became Industrial Correspondent, then News Editor. Moved to London as Assistant Editor, *TV News* and later (1977) Editor. Now Assistant Director-General.

Sheelagh Rees. Joined TV from radio in 1946 as production secretary. In early 1950s joined Wolf Rilla, when they were sole staff of Script Section as it was then. Became first woman Floor Manager, working with various directors on mainly live productions. During this time also directed documentaries. Before retiring was production associate on *To Serve Them All My Days* and *Mansfield Park*.

Alan Richardson. Joined TV *Newsreel* at AP in 1948 as Film Librarian, following Navy war service. Later became Telerecording Manager. Wrote and directed the 10th Anniversary of Eurovision programme. Since retiring has become a West Country Tourist Board Guide and a Director of Salisbury Playhouse.

Paddy Russell. Actress and freelance Stage Manager in the fifties, for twelve years was Rudi Cartier's SM and later Unit Manager/FM. Became freelance director; worked on *Dr Who*, *Z-Cars* and *Softly, Softly*. Directed two of *Late Night Horror* plays first recorded in colour. Has directed for LWT, Thames, Granada and Yorkshire, directing situation comedy including two series of *My Old Man* with Clive Dunn. Currently is a director at Yorkshire TV.

Maggie Saunders. Joined BBC-TV in 1948 from the European Service. Worked on such early series as the Cyril Fletcher shows and the *Hulbert Follies*, when the afternoon show was repeated in the evening. Moved to Music Department and worked with Beecham, Barbirolli and Sargent. Assistant Floor Manager from 1953 until early retirement in 1977, with spells as Floor Manager and vision mixer, with Children's plays and the *Black and White Minstrel Show*.

Michael Scott. Joined Rank Organisation on leaving public school awaiting training as film editor. Overheard producer Eric Fawcett interviewing staff for commercial TV and changed course: became a trainee FM with Screen Services. Joined Granada. Became producer/presenter on their daily programme. Is now Programme Controller, Granada TV.

Jane Scrase-Dickins. Was one of first costume designers taken on in fifties from Sadlers Wells. Worked on ballet productions and some drama. Designed for the Silhouettes over five years including the Bill Cotton Band Show appearances. Left to marry. A qualified Member of the Embroiderers Guild, has become known for her embroidered boxes. One was presented to the Queen.

Bob Service. Was sound radio engineer until 1944 when served in REME until fifties when he returned to BBC. Joined AR in 1955 as trainee cameraman. Became OB Director in 1969 with Thames TV. Directed varied programmes including royal OBs. Is now director in Further Education Department.

Vera Seton-Reid. Joined BBC Engineering as technical assistant. Moved to TV as a vision-mixer, one of the original team. Worked with many drama and LE producers. As TV developed, worked at Riverside, Lime Grove studios and TV Centre, moving to Bush House as studio manager until retirement.

Chris Sharpe. Trained as an art teacher, then worked as a designer in advertising. Worked on many early TV commercials such as 'Hartley's New Jam' and 'People Love Players'. Now a partner in an advertising agency.

John Summers. Joined BBC TV as a camera assistant on tests before re-start. Became a cameraman at AP; whilst on OBs was a cameraman for *Calais en Fête*, the first OB from outside Britain. Returned to studio and has now been Lighting Director for 30 of his 39 years in TV. Was awarded the 1985 Royal Television Society Silver Medal, the first time the award has been given to a craftsman.

Brian Tesler. Won a state scholarship to Oxford but served with Forces Broadcasting in Trieste before taking up his studies. While at Oxford ran an experimental theatre. Joined BBC TV as a general trainee in LE graduating to producer. Joined ITV and became Controller of Programmes Thames TV. Ten years ago joined LWT where he is now Chairman. RTS Vice-president.

Simon Theobalds. Came into television from the Army, having served in the Royal Green Jackets for ten years, before joining Southern Television in 1971 as an editorial assistant; then became a reporter on *Day by Day*. Later moved to become Head of Press and PR with Southern. Is currently Public Relations Manager for TVS.

Hugh Tosh. Joined BBC in 1939 as a librarian; later became a stills photographer, moving to AP in 1947 and then TV Design Department. Worked on *Z-Cars* and *Softly, Softly*, doing back projection stills, and for *Maigret*, *Civilisation*, *Royal Ascot* and *All Your Own*, among many programmes, taking literally thousands of production pictures. Is now retired.

Steve Wade. Joined BBC TV 1938. After wartime RAF rejoined as a cameraman. Transferred to OBs as their first Stage Manager when you were allowed 1s for lunch and 2d for the loo on location at, say, Ascot. Moved to ATV and headed their OB department. Later Head OBs at Southern TV. Is now retired but tutors trainee director courses for ITCA at Bristol University.

Bill Ward OBE. Joined before the start of television as one of the first six technicians. Returned post-war as a studio manager, was made a producer by Cecil McGivern. Moved in 1955 to ATV as Head of LE, recruited by Lew Grade on the advice of Bob Hope. Later appointed to Board of ATV. EBU Executive for major sporting events. Presented with 1976 Desmond Davis award. Fellow of RSA.

Beryl Watts. Joined BBC radio in Bristol in 1943. Moved to TV ten years later. Worked first as producer's secretary to guest producers and then with Hal Burton and Tony Richardson. Then worked as assistant to Rudolph Cartier and Gil Calder, and latterly for freelance directors in Drama.

Cyril Wilkins. Joined BBC as a technical assistant in Manchester 1936. Moved to TV as one of first six engineers pre-war. Became camera tracker and then leader of one of the first two camera crews. Returned to TV after war and became senior cameraman. Is now retired.

David Wilson. Was on the board of A-R as Director and adviser to the Managing Director, and moved over to Southern TV at its inception in 1957 as Managing Director, and as its Chairman in 1976 until the company's demise in 1981.

Maureen Winslade. Was junior make-up assistant at AP, moving to Lime Grove doing make-up on LE shows, opera, ballet and music. In at the start of *Z-Cars* working on that and drama serials until becoming Assistant Head of Make-up. Was member of colour training team.

Bob Wright. Joined radio engineering 1944. Went to AP in 1949 as a camera tracker. Became a lighting director when controls were primitive and every lamp was on a block and tackle. Lit *The Six Wives of Henry VIII, The Forsyte Saga, Elizabeth R* and many LE shows including *Whacko*. Now Head of Lighting, and has instigated and developed the BBC's video effects workshop.

Michael Yates. Joined TV at Lime Grove 1950 after training in USA and design at Royal Opera House. Designed Children's productions, especially ballet. Became Head of Design at A-R at start of ITV. Designed important productions including *Laudes Evangelii* and *Midsummer Night's Dream.* In 1968 became Head of Design LWT until he retired.

Index of People and Programmes

Numbers in italics refer to illustrations

STOCKTON - BILLINGHAM

LIBRARY

TECHNICAL COLLEGE